D1557993
Martin Storey's
afghan knits

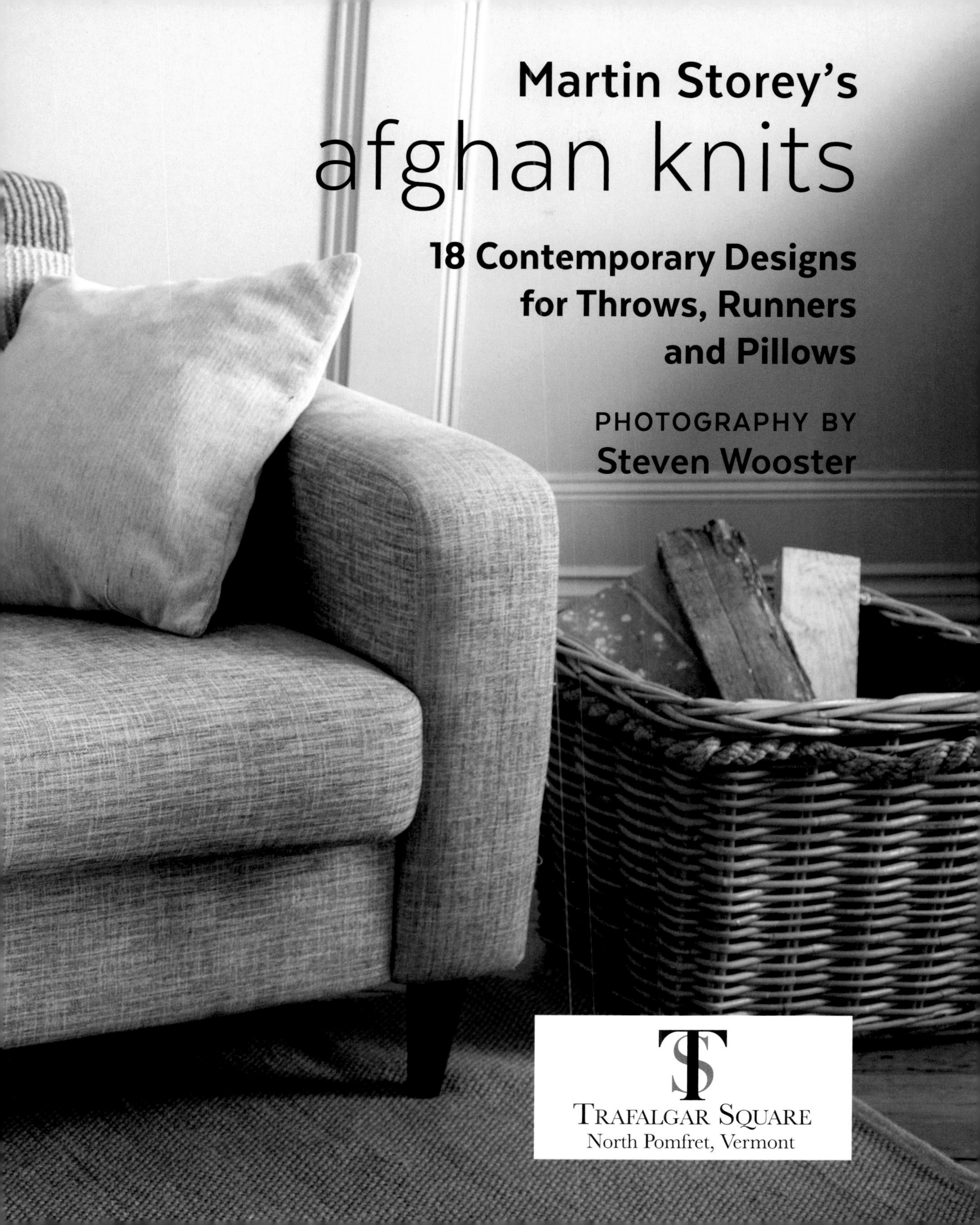

Martin Storey's afghan knits

18 Contemporary Designs for Throws, Runners and Pillows

PHOTOGRAPHY BY
Steven Wooster

TRAFALGAR SQUARE
North Pomfret, Vermont

Martin Storey's Afghan Knits
First published in the USA in 2017
by Trafalgar Square Books
North Pomfret
Vermont 05053

Copyright © Berry & Co (Publishing) Ltd 2016
Designs copyright © Martin Storey 2016

All rights reserved. No part of this publication may be recorded, stored in a retrieval system or transmitted in any form or by any means, electronic, electrostatic, magnetic tape, mechanical, photocopying, recording or otherwise, without the prior permission in writing from the publishers.

The instructions and material lists in this book were carefully reviewed by the author and editor. However accuracy cannot be guaranteed and the author and publisher cannot be held liable for any errors.

Design: Anne Wilson
Pattern writing (and knitting): Martin Storey
Pattern editing/checking: Lisa Richardson
Charts: Anne Wilson
Diagrams: Ed Berry
Styling: Susan Berry

ISBN 978-1-57076-862-0
Library of Congress Contol Number: 2017946802

Printed in China

contents

introduction

One of the reasons I love designing and knitting Afghans is the wonderful flexibility they offer: because the patterns are so straightforward, you can go to town on a great range of textured stitches or brilliant colorways, or a combination of the two. Another good reason is that projects composed of Afghan squares or strips are so portable: you can knit on trains, boats and planes, in your lunch break or on the beach, your knitting project fitting conveniently into a small bag. For knitting addicts, what could be more enticing and for novice knitters, what could be simpler?

My aim in this book is to provide designs with a contemporary twist: the kind of projects that add personality or a touch of glamor to an otherwise relatively plain décor. I have included some, like the Creative Cables throw, that provide knitters with some stitch patterns to get their teeth into while others, like the Beach Stripes blanket and mat, are easy enough for novice knitters to manage.

I hope very much that you will use my designs in this book as a starting point for experimenting with your own combinations of stitch and color or even of scale. Nothing could be simpler than to turn them into a much bigger throw, for example, or perhaps a bedside rug, by choosing a thicker yarn and bigger needles.

I hope you have as much fun knitting the projects in this book as I have had in designing them!

color blocks blanket

Knitted in garter stitch in four toning colorways of Rowan *Felted Tweed* (or *Pure Wool Superwash Worsted*) this blanket is made up of 63 squares - 20 plain, 12 with a dark blue border and pale gray center, and 31 with a pale gray border and mid-blue center. Each square is cleverly worked by the k2tog and k3tog decreases (the diagonal lines seen in each square); then the final square is formed by joining together the row-end edges. Pattern on page 46.

color blocks pillow

Made from similar squares to the Color Blocks blanket on page 8, and in the same yarns, this design consists of 9 squares, with the central square the only plain square, and 4 of the remaining 8 squares with a dark green border and gray center, and the remaining 4 with a gray border and brown center. Pattern on page 48.

creative cables throw

This throw is a treat for anyone who loves knitting cables, as it comprises six different cable patterns, in seven different colorways, knitted in Rowan *Pure Wool Superwash Worsted*. Pattern on page 50.

simply stripes pillow

This lovely toning rectangular pillow is created from 12 squares of a ridged garter-stitch design, with each square employing a stone-colored stripe with another colorway, all knitted in Rowan *Felted Tweed*. Pattern on page 56.

simply stripes blanket

This is a larger version of the Simply Stripes pillow, using 63 squares (9 deep and 7 wide). The flecked Rowan *Felted Tweed* yarn creates a lovely tonal yet bright design, which helps to add texture and color to a simple sofa. Pattern on page 56.

wintry blanket

This features two lovely chunky cable designs in Rowan *Big Wool* offset by narrower cable stripes, made in three strips. It would make a great end-of-bed throw if you increased the length. Pattern on page 59.

winter trees pillow

Another very pretty lacy design, using two different lace motifs, knitted in either Rowan *Alpaca Color* with its natural soft striping or in *Felted Tweed* or *Pure Wool Superwash DK*. As with the Springtime pillow (see page 32), the lacy motifs are centred in a square edged with garter stitch. Pattern on page 62.

little folk pillow

This charming little pillow employs nine different motifs knitted in two colors only in either Rowan *Wool Cotton 4 ply* or *Summerlite 4 ply* making it relatively simple to work. Four geometric motifs combine with a little rabbit, bee, heart and elephant that would look great in a child's nursery too. Pattern on page 66.

little folk blanket

And here are the same nine motifs as the pillow (see page 22), knitted in the same yarns, but this time joined together to form a crib blanket: 7 squares long by 6 squares wide, finished with a narrow contrasting garter trim. Pattern on page 70.

modern art blanket

Knitted in Rowan *Pure Wool Worsted* garter stitch in five differently colored strips, this very simple blanket is also very effective. You can choose from this version in seven colors or a more monochrome version in six colors (overleaf). Pattern on page 72.

icelandic pillow

And this pillow is a similar treat for those who like knitting colorwork designs! And, with just two colors in a row, and two different designs, it is simpler to knit than it looks. Knitted in Rowan *Felted Tweed Aran*. Pattern on page 74.

springtime pillow

This is ideal for those who want a little lacy project that is relatively easy to work. With its “hearts and flowers” design, it requires five “flower” and four “heart” blocks to complete the pillow top. Each block is knitted in stockinette stitch with a narrow garter stitch border. Knitted in Rowan *Summerlite 4ply*. Pattern on page 80.

springtime blanket

A larger version of the pillow (see page 32), this blanket requires 63 squares to be made – 32 “flowers” and 31 “hearts”. You could, if you wish, translate this design into a light summer wrap by making it longer and narrower. Knitted in Rowan *Summerlite 4ply*. Pattern on page 76.

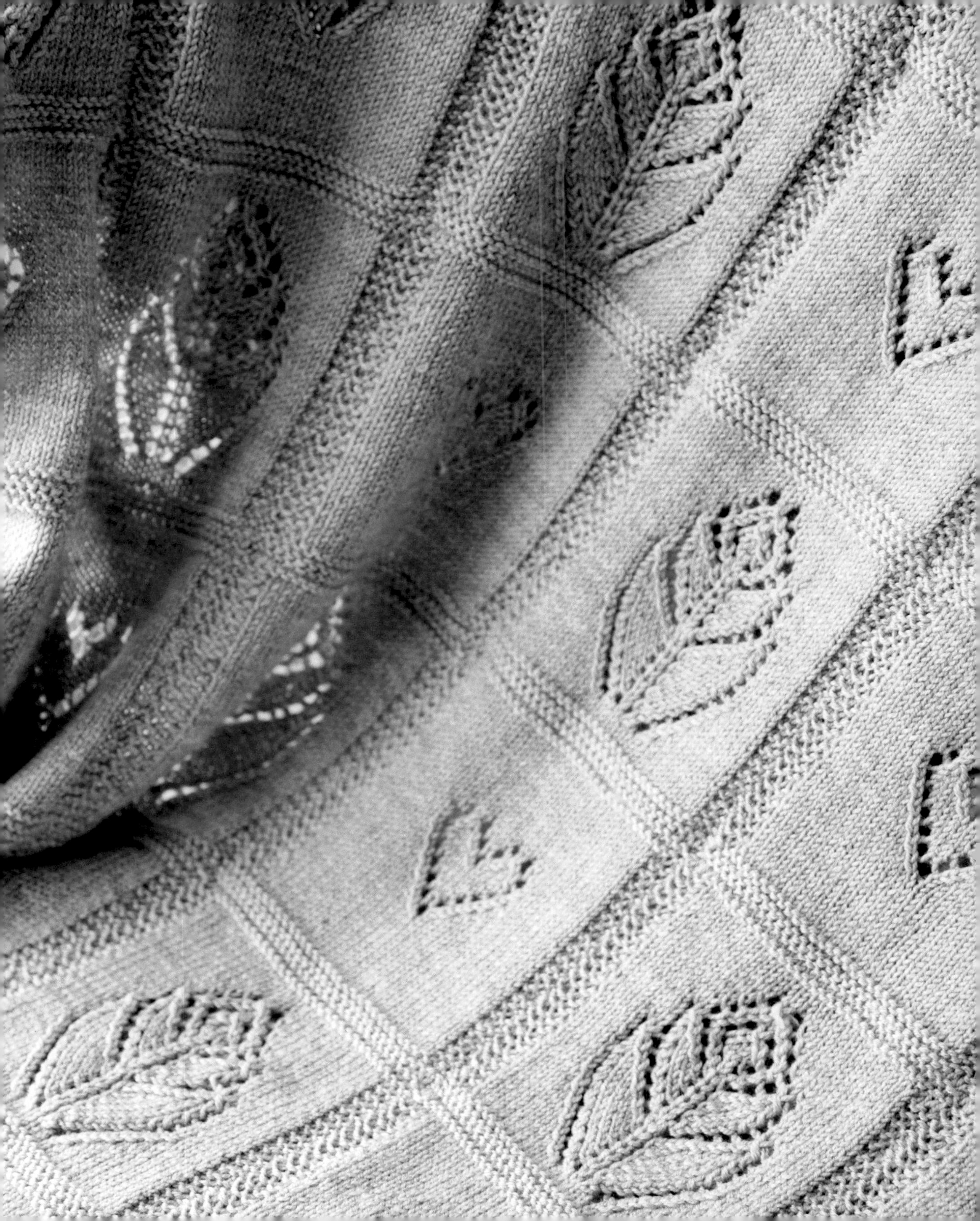

beach stripes blanket

This is knitted in four garter stitch strips using three different designs, the first one being repeated for the fourth. Knitted in 9 different colorways of Rowan *Wool Cotton* or *Handknit Cotton*, its impact is gained from the different stripe combinations that make up each strip. Pattern on page 81.

7461
PANTONE
UNIVERSE™
376

beach stripes mat

Knitted in the same yarns as the Beach Stripes blanket (see page 36), this makes a great table or serving-tray mat – the perfect first colorwork project for a novice knitter. A narrow garter stitch edging makes a simple and attractive finishing touch. Pattern on page 84.

sunset pillow

A similarly two-tone textured design to the Simply Stripes pillow and blanket (see pages 14 and 16), this employs the Intarsia technique to create the central ridge and striped circle blocks, of which 9 are needed to make up the pillow. Knitted in Rowan *Pure Wool Superwash Worsted*. Pattern on page 86.

autumn leaves throw

Small stockinette stitch squares in 8 different colorways of Rowan *Felted Tweed* create the base for this rectangular throw to which 8 different garter-stitch leaf shapes, some striped and some plain, have been appliquéd. A similar leaf shape forms the trim, knitted in a ninth color. The throw is 8 squares long by 4 squares wide. Pattern on page 88.

autumn leaves runner

A similar design to the throw on page 42, this little mat or runner is created from a similar set of 8 squares and leaves in *Felted Tweed*, with or without a simple garter-stitch trim. The 8 blocks (right) show which leaf sits on which colored square. Pattern on page 91.

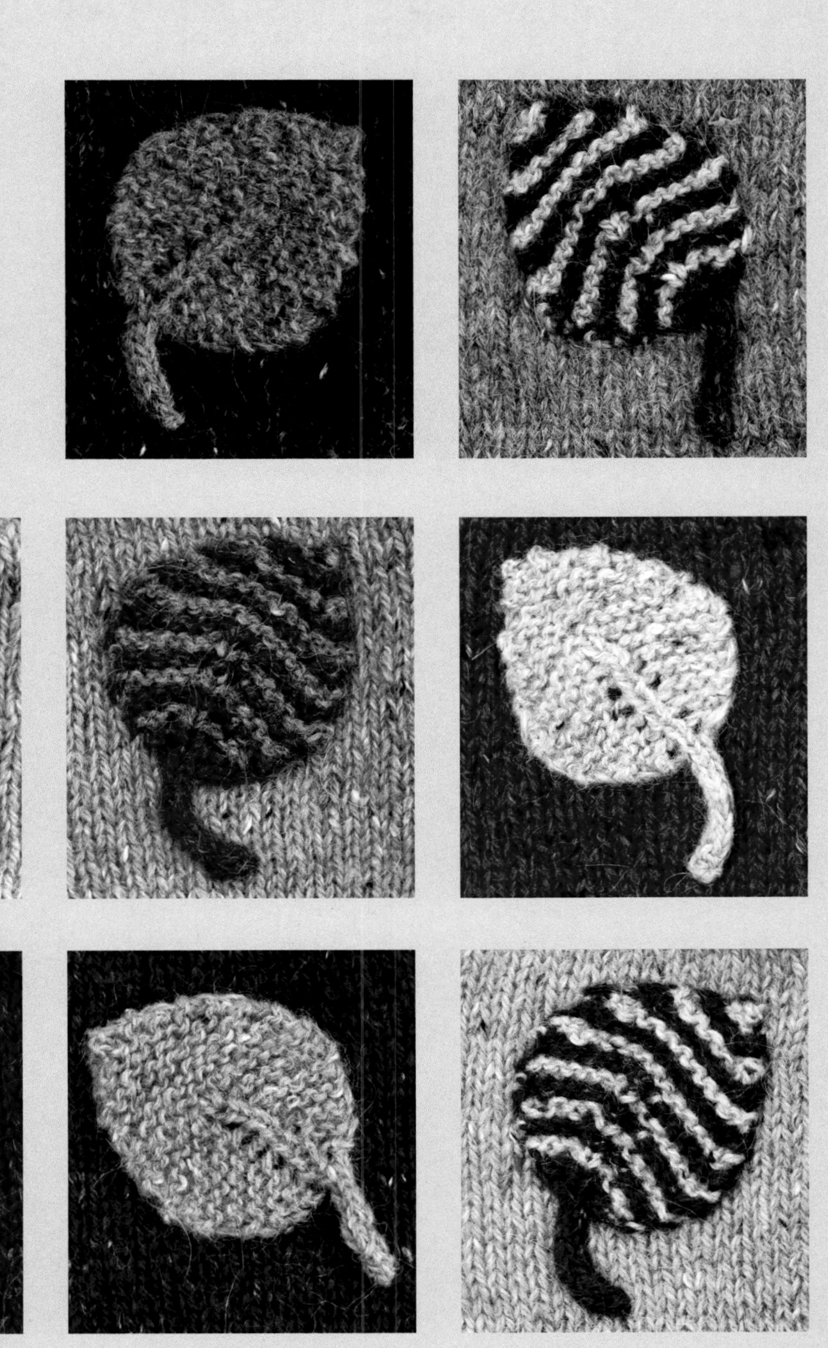

color blocks blanket

YARN

Creative Focus Worsted

A	Nickel	00401	4 x 3½oz/220yd
B	Marine	01660	1 x 3½oz/220yd
C	Delft	01321	2 x 3½oz/220yd
D	Teal	03360	3 x 3½oz/220yd

OR

Pure Wool Superwash Worsted

A	Moonstone	112	4 x 3½oz/219yd
B	Navy	149	1 x 3½oz/219yd
C	Electric	143	2 x 13½oz/219yd
D	Mallard	144	3 x 3½oz/219yd

NEEDLES

1 pair US 7 (4.5 mm) needles

GAUGE

20 sts and 24 rows to 4 in (10 cm) square measured over stockinette stitch using US 7 (4.5 mm) needles, or size required to obtain correct gauge.

FINISHED SIZE

Blanket measures approx 33 in (84 cm) x 42½ in (108 cm).

ABBREVIATIONS

See page 93.

BLANKET

BLOCK 1 [make 12]

Cast on 89 sts using US 7 (4.5mm) needles and yarn B.

Foundation row: K to end.

Row 1 (RS): K2tog, [k19, k3tog] 3 times, k19, k2tog. *81sts*

Row 2 and every alt row: Knit.

Row 3: K2tog, [k17, k3tog] 3 times, k17, k2tog. *73sts*

Row 5: K2tog, [k15, k3tog] 3 times, k17, k2tog. *65sts*

Row 7: K2tog, [k13, k3tog] 3 times, k17, k2tog. *57sts*

Row 8: Knit.

Fasten off yarn B and join in yarn A. Now working in yarn A throughout cont working patt as set, working 2 less K sts between each decrease on every RS row until 9sts remain.

Next row: [k3tog] 3 times. *3sts*

Next row: K3tog and fasten off.

Join seam to form a square.

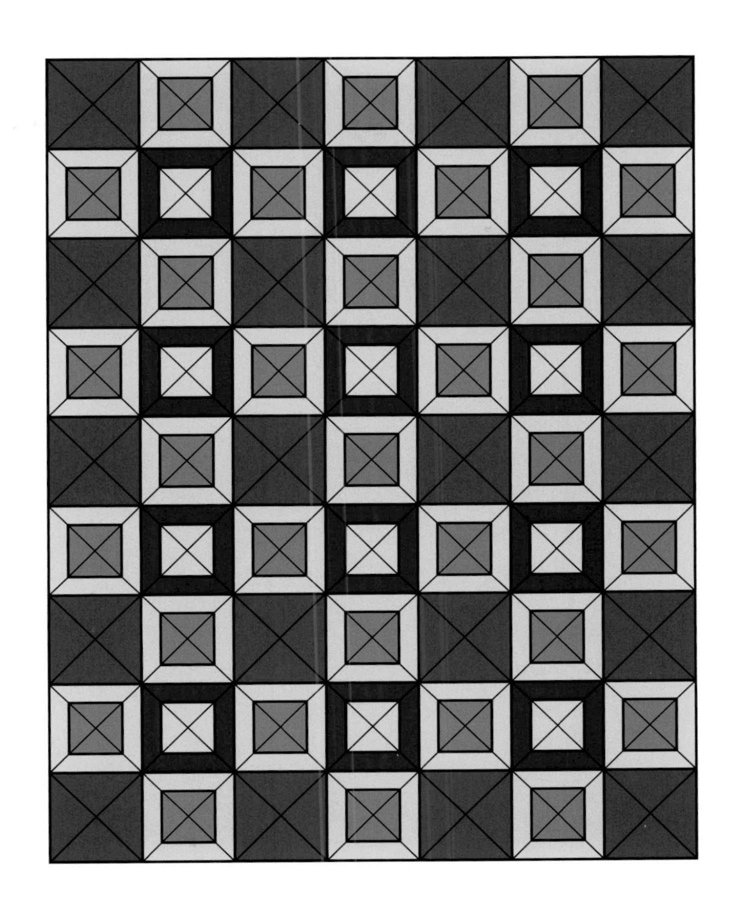

BLOCK 2 [make 31]

Work as Block 1 using yarn A in place of yarn B (foundation row and next 8 rows), and yarn C in place of yarn A.

BLOCK 3 [make 20]

Work as Block 1 using yarn D throughout.

FINISHING

Join blocks as shown on sketch, to form a large rectangle 7 blocks wide and 9 blocks long [63 blocks in total].

color blocks pillow

YARN

Creative Focus Worsted

A	Nickel	00401	1 x 3½oz/220yd
B	Basil	01350	1 x 3½oz/220yd
C	Golden Heather	00018	1 x 3½oz/220yd
D	New Fern	01265	1 x 3½oz/220yd

OR

Pure Wool Superwash Worsted

A	Moonstone	112	1 x 3½oz/219yd
B	Hawthorn	141	1 x 3½oz/219yd
C	Rust	106	1 x 3½oz/219yd
D	Olive	125	1 x 3½oz/219yd

NEEDLES

1 pair US 7 (4.5 mm) needles

EXTRAS

14 in (35 cm) square pillow form

15½ in (39 cm) square of backing fabric

GAUGE

20 sts and 24 rows to 4 in (10 cm) square measured over stockinette stitch using US 7 (4.5 mm) needles, or size required to obtain correct gauge.

FINISHED SIZE

Pillow measures approx 14 in x 14 in (35 cm x 35 cm)

ABBREVIATIONS

See page 93.

PILLOW FRONT

BLOCK 1 [make 4]

Cast on 89 sts using US 7 (4.5 mm) needles and yarn B.

Foundation row: K to end.

Row 1 (RS): K2tog, [k19, k3tog] 3 times, k19, k2tog. *81sts*

Row 2 and every alt row: Knit.

Row 3: K2tog, [k17, k3tog] 3 times, k17, k2tog. *73sts*

Row 5: K2tog, [k15, k3tog] 3 times, k17, k2tog. *65sts*

Row 7: K2tog, [k13, k3tog] 3 times, k17, k2tog. *57sts*

Row 8: Knit.

Fasten off yarn B and join in yarn A. Now working in yarn A throughout cont working patt as set, working 2 less K sts between each decrease on every RS row until 9sts remain.

Next row: [k3tog] 3 times. *3sts*

Next row: K3tog and fasten off.

Join seam to form a square.

BLOCK 2 [make 4]

Work as Block 1 using yarn A in place of yarn B (foundation row and next 8 rows) and yarn C in place of yarn A.

BLOCK 3 [make 1]

Work as Block 1 using yarn D throughout.

FINISHING

To form Pillow front: Join blocks as shown on sketch, to form a large square 3 blocks wide and 3 blocks long [9 blocks in total].
Trim backing fabric to same size as knitted section, adding seam allowance along all edges. Fold ½ in (1 cm) seam allowance to WS along all edges of backing fabric. Lay backing fabric onto knitted piece with WS facing and sew backing fabric in place along 3 sides. Insert pillow form, then close 4th side.

creative cables throw

YARN

Pure Wool Superwash Worsted

A	Granite	111	2 x 3½oz/219yd
B	Damson	150	2 x 3½oz/219yd
C	Apple	129	3 x 3½oz/219yd
D	Mallard	144	2 x 3½oz/219yd
E	Oak	159	2 x 3½oz/219yd
F	Soft Cream	102	2 x 3½oz/219yd
G	Chestnut	107	3 x 3½oz/219yd
OR			
A	Granite	111	2 x 3½oz/219yd
B/G	Damson	150	5 x 3½oz/219yd
C	Olive	125	3 x 3½oz/219yd
D	Mallard	144	2 x 3½oz/219yd
E	Rust	106	2 x 13½oz/219yd
F	Soft Cream	102	2 x 3½oz/219yd

NEEDLES

1 pair US 7 (4.5 mm) and US 6 (4 mm) needles
1 cable needle

GAUGE

19 sts and 25 rows to 4 in (10 cm) square measured over stockinette stitch using US 7 (4.5 mm) needles, or size required to obtain correct gauge.

FINISHED SIZE

Throw measures approx 45½ in (115 cm) x 59 in (150 cm)

ABBREVIATIONS

c4r = slip next st onto cable needle and hold at back of work, k3, then p1 from cable needle.
c4l = slip next 3 sts onto cable needle and hold at front of work, p1, then k3 from cable needle.
t4r = slip next st onto cable needle and hold at back of work, k3, then k1 from cable needle.
t4l = slip next 3 sts onto cable needle and hold at front of work, k1, then k3 from cable needle.
tw4r = slip next 2 sts onto cable needle and hold at back of work, k2, then p2 from cable needle.
tw4l = slip next 2 sts onto cable needle and hold at front of work, p2, then k2 from cable needle.
c5r = slip next 2 sts onto cable needle and hold at back of work, k3, then p2 from cable needle.
c5l = slip next 3 sts onto cable needle and hold at front of work, p2, then k3 from cable needle.
c4b[f] = slip next 2 sts on to a cable needle and hold in back [front] of work, k2 then k2 from cable needle.
c6b[f] = slip next 3 sts on to a cable needle and hold in back [front] of work, k3 then k3 from cable needle.
cr7b = slip next 4 sts on to a cable needle and hold in back of work, k3 then k4 from cable needle.
c8b = slip next 4 sts on to a cable needle and hold in back of work, k4 then k4 from cable needle.
make bobble = [K1, p1, k1] all into next st, turn, p3, turn, k3, turn p3, turn sl1K, k2tog, psso.
See also page 93.

NOTE

When working from Charts, right side rows are read from right to left; wrong side rows are read from left to right.

THROW

CABLE STRIP 1

Cast on 38 sts using US 7 (4.5 mm) needles and yarn A.

Cont to work from Chart 1, beg at bottom right hand corner [1st row is RS of work].

Work the 16 row patt rep 24 times, ending with RS facing for next row. *384 rows.*

Bind off.

CABLE STRIP 2

Cast on 45 sts using US 7 (4.5 mm) needles and yarn B.

Cont to work from Chart 2, beg at bottom right hand corner [1st row is RS of work].

Work the 24 row patt rep 16 times, ending with RS facing for next row. *384 rows.*

Bind off.

CABLE STRIP 3

Cast on 38 sts using US 7 (4.5 mm) needles and yarn C.

Cont to work from Chart 3, beg at bottom right hand corner [1st row is RS of work].

Work the 12 row patt rep 32 times, ending with RS facing for next row. *384 rows.*

Bind off.

CABLE STRIPS 1 AND 7

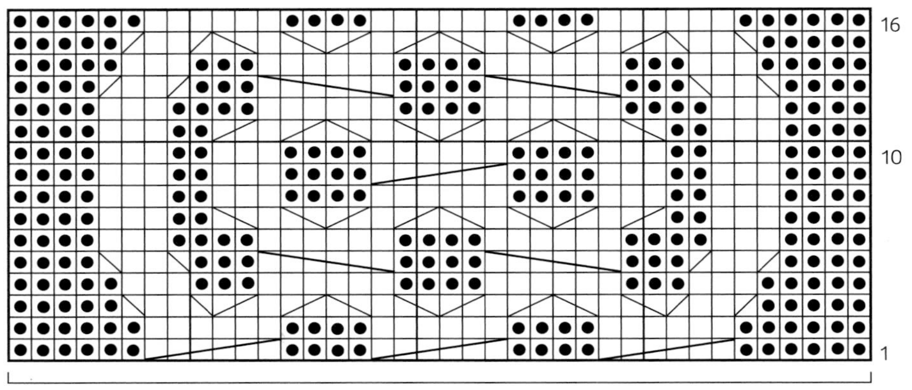

CABLE STRIP 2

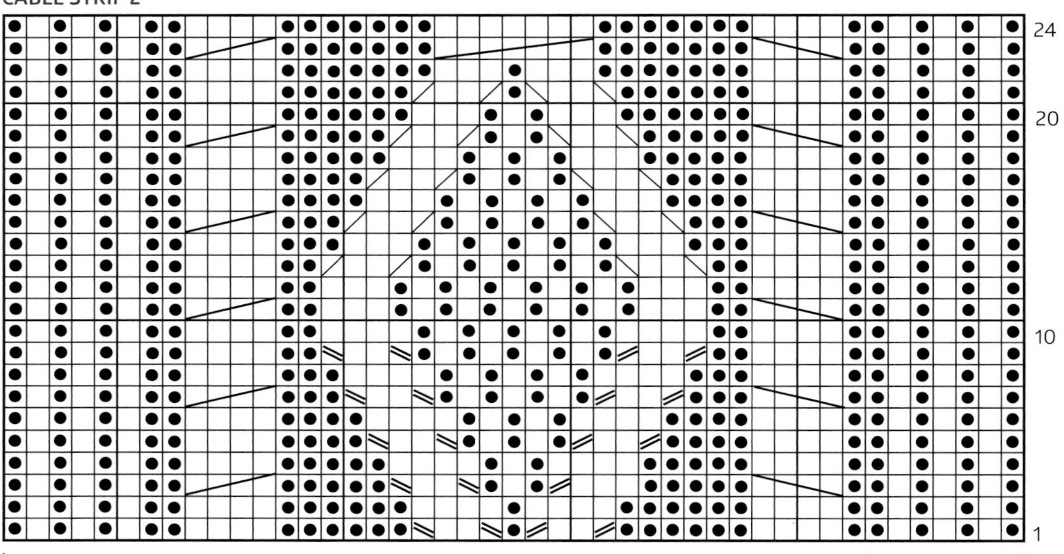

CABLE STRIP 3

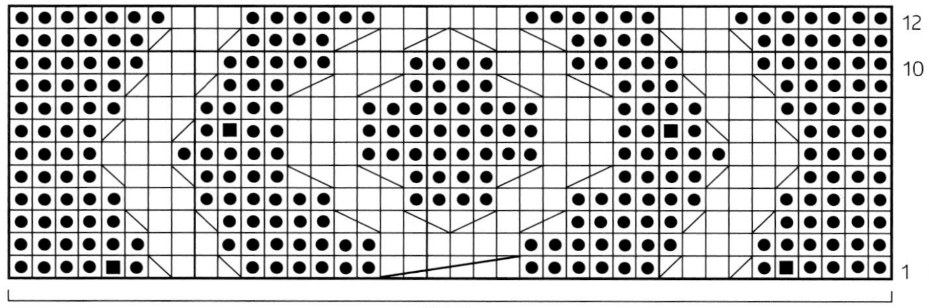

CABLE STRIP 4

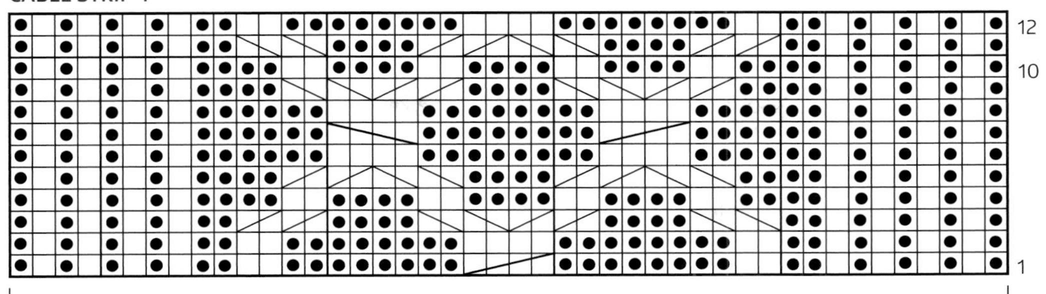

CABLE STRIP 5

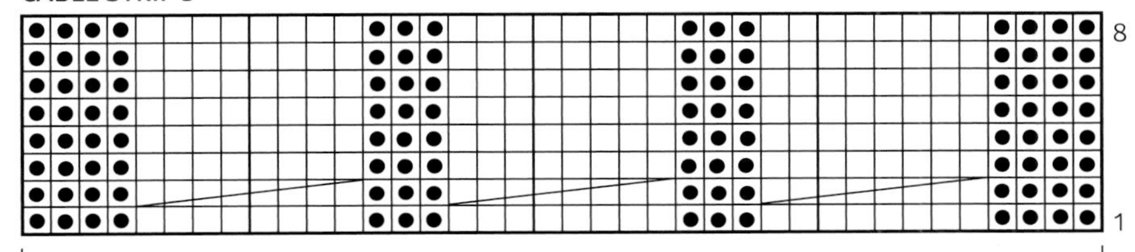

CABLE STRIP 6

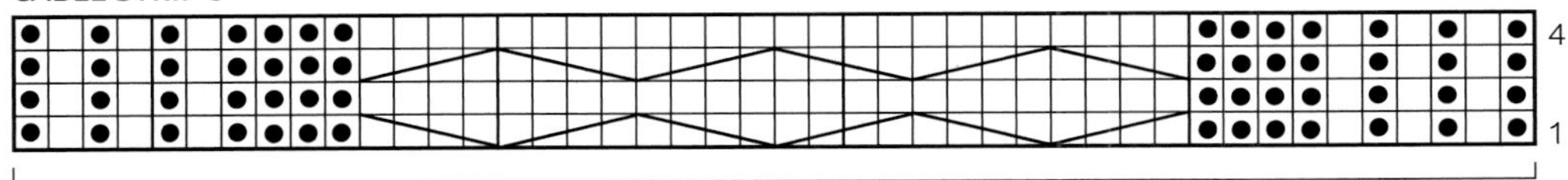

KEY

- K on RS, P on WS
- P on RS, K on WS
- c4r
- c4l
- c4b
- c4f
- t4r
- t4l
- tw4r
- tw4l
- c5r
- c5l
- c6b
- c6f
- cr7b
- c8b
- make bobble

CABLE STRIP 4

Cast on 44 sts using US 7 (4.5 mm) needles and yarn D.
Cont to work from Chart 4, beg at bottom right hand corner [1st row is RS of work].
Work the 12 row patt rep 32 times, ending with RS facing for next row. *384 rows.*
Bind off.

CABLE STRIP 5

Cast on 38 sts using US 7 (4.5 mm) needles and yarn E.
Cont to work from Chart 5, beg at bottom right hand corner [1st row is RS of work].
Work the 8 row patt rep 48 times, ending with RS facing for next row. *384 rows.*
Bind off.

CABLE STRIP 6

Cast on 44 sts using US 7 (4.5 mm) needles and yarn F.
Cont to work from Chart 6, beg at bottom right hand corner [1st row is RS of work].
Work the 4 row patt rep 96 times, ending with RS facing for next row. *384 rows.*
Bind off.

CABLE STRIP 7

Cast on 38 sts using US 7 (4.5 mm) needles and yarn G.
Cont to work from Chart of Cable Strip 1, beg at bottom right hand corner [1st row is RS of work].
Work the 16 row patt rep 24 times, ending with RS facing for next row. *384 rows.*
Bind off.

FINISHING

Mattress stitch or slip stitch all 7 strips neatly together as shown on sketch and in order to form one large rectangle.

SIDE EDGINGS [both alike]

Cast on 13 sts using US 6 (4 mm) needles and yarn G.
Always twisting yarns together at right hand edge of work when changing color and passing the darker color over the lighter color, cont in stripe garter stitch pattern as follows:-
Row 1 (RS): Using yarn C.
Row 2: Using yarn C.
Row 3: Using yarn G.
Row 4: Using yarn G.
These 4 rows form the stripe garter stitch pattern.
Cont to rep these 4 rows until work, when slightly stretched, fits up one entire row end edge of blanket and ending on a 3rd pattern row, WS facing for next row.
Next row (WS): Using yarn G, bind off knitwise [on WS]
Repeat for opposite side edge.
Slip stitch or mattress stitch side edgings into place.

TOP EDGING

Cast on 13 sts using US 6 (4 mm) needles and yarn G.
Cont in stripe garter stitch pattern until work, when slightly stretched, fits along entire top edge of blanket and across both short ends of side edgings and ending on a 3rd pattern row, WS facing for next row.
Next row (WS): Using yarn G, bind off knitwise [on WS].
Slip stitch or mattress stitch top edging into place.

BOTTOM EDGING

Repeat as for top edging.

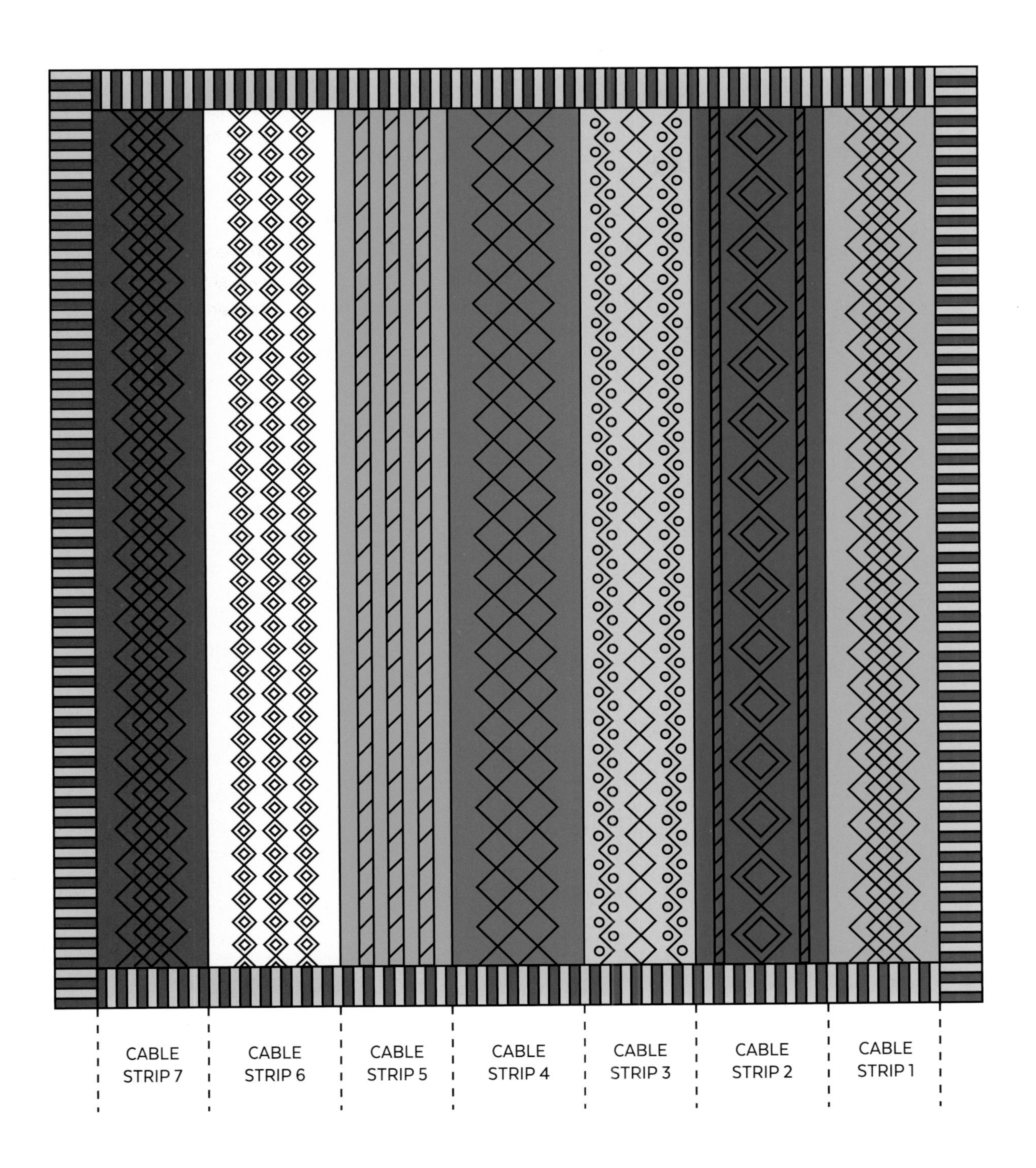
CABLE STRIP 7
CABLE STRIP 6
CABLE STRIP 5
CABLE STRIP 4
CABLE STRIP 3
CABLE STRIP 2
CABLE STRIP 1

simply stripes blanket and pillow

YARN

Felted Tweed

Blanket

A	Stone	190	4 x 1¾oz/131yd balls

Cushion

A	Stone	190	1 x 1¾oz/131yd ball

1 x 1¾oz/131yd ball of each of the following shades will be adequate to work both projects.

B	Ginger	154
C	Mineral	181
D	Maritime	167
E	Peony	183
F	Avocado	161
G	Seafarer	170
H	Bilberry	151
I	Pine	158
J	Seasalter	178
K	Rage	150
L	Treacle	145
M	Watery	152

NEEDLES

1 pair US 5 (3.75 mm) needles.

EXTRAS

Pillow only - 12 in (30 cm) x 15½ in (40 cm) pillow form and 13½ in (34cm) x 17½ in (44 cm) rectangle of backing fabric.

GAUGE

23 sts and 38 rows to 4in (10 cm)measured over garter ridge stitch using US 5 (3.75 mm) needles, or size required to obtain correct gauge.

FINISHED SIZE

Blanket measures approx 27½ in (70 cm) x 35½ in (90 cm)
Pillow measures approx. 12 in (30 cm) x 15½ in (40 cm)

ABBREVIATIONS

See page 93.

1	2	3	1	2	3	1
4	5	6	4	5	6	4
7	8	9	7	8	9	7
10	11	12	10	11	12	10
1	2	3	1	2	3	1
4	5	6	4	5	6	4
7	8	9	7	8	9	7
10	11	12	10	11	12	10
1	2	3	1	2	3	1

BLANKET

SQUARE 1 [make 9]

Cast on 23 sts using US 5 (3.75 mm) needles and yarn A.
Row 1 (RS): Using yarn A, knit.
Row 2: Using yarn A, purl.
Row 3: Using yarn B, knit.
Row 4: Using yarn B, knit.
These 4 rows form the garter ridge pattern.
Repeat these 4 rows 8 times more, carrying colors not in use up side of work.
Row 37 (RS): Using yarn A, knit.
Row 38: Using yarn A, purl.
Cast off knitwise.

SQUARES 2 TO 12

With A as the main [cast-on] color, make a further 54 blocks as folls:-
Square 2 [make 6]: Repeat using colors A and C.
Square 3 [make 6]: Repeat using colors A and D.
Square 4 [make 6]: Repeat using colors A and E.
Square 5 [make 4]: Repeat using colors A and F.
Square 6 [make 4]: Repeat using colors A and G.
Square 7 [make 6]: Repeat using colors A and H.
Square 8 [make 4]: Repeat using colors A and I.
Square 9 [make 4]: Repeat using colors A and J.
Square 10 [make 6]: Repeat using colors A and K.
Square 11 [make 4]: Repeat using colors A and L.
Square 12 [make 4]: Repeat using colors A and M.
Total = 63 Squares

FINISHING

Using back stitch or mattress stitch if preferred, join all 63 squares, as shown by grid, to form a large rectangle 7 squares wide and 9 squares long.

PILLOW

Work 1 square of each colorway as detailed on pages 56-7.
Total = 12 Squares

FINISHING

Using back stitch or mattress stitch if preferred, join all 12 squares, as shown by grid, to form a large rectangle 3 squares wide and 4 squares long.
Trim backing fabric to same size as knitted section adding a seam allowance along all edges. Fold seam allowance to WS along all edges of backing fabric. Lay backing fabric onto knitted piece with WS facing and sew backing fabric in place along 3 sides. Insert pillow form, then close 4th side.

1	2	3
4	5	6
7	8	9
10	11	12

wintry blanket

YARN

Big Wool

Concrete 061 23 x 3½oz/87yd

NEEDLES

1 pair US 15 (10 mm) needles

1 cable needle

GAUGE

9 sts and 12.5 rows to 4 in (10 cm) measured over stockinette stitch using US 15 (10 mm) needles, or size required to obtain correct gauge.

FINISHED SIZE

Blanket measures approx 40 in (102mm) x 90½ in (230 cm).

ABBREVIATIONS

c6b[f] = slip next 3 sts on to a cable needle and hold in back [front] of work, k3 then k3 from cable needle.
m1 = make one stitch by inserting needle from behind under the running thread (which is the strand running from the base of the stitch just worked to the base of the next stitch) and lift this thread onto the left hand needle, then knit one stitch into the back of it on RS, purl one stitch into the back on WS.
See also page 93.

NOTE

When working from Charts, right side rows are read from right to left; wrong side rows are read from left to right.

BLANKET

CABLE STRIP 1

Cast on 38 sts using US 15 (10mm) needles.

Row 1 (RS): (P1, K1) twice, P4, (K2, P2) 5 times, K2, P4, (K1, P1) twice.

Row 2: (K1, P1) twice, K4, P2, (K2, P2) 5 times, K4, (P1, K1) twice.

The last 2 rows sets the rib patt, rep the last 2 rows once more then row 1 again.

Row 6 (WS): (K1, P1) twice, K4, P2, K2, P2, K1, m1, K1, m1, P1, m1, P1, m1, K2, m1, P1, m1, P1, m1, K1, m1, K1, P2, K2, P2, K4, (P1, K1) twice. *46 sts.*

Cont to work from Chart, beg at bottom right hand corner [1st row is RS of work].

Work the 8-row patt rep 38 times, then rows 1 to 7 once ending with WS facing for next row.

311 rows of chart worked.

Next row (WS): (K1, P1) twice, K4, P6, (p2tog) 4 times, P2, (p2tog) 4times, P6, K4, (P1, K1) twice. *38 sts.*

Work the rib patt as set for 6 rows ending with RS facing for next row.

Bind off in rib.

CABLE STRIP 2 (make 2)

Cast on 38 sts using US 15 (10mm) needles.

Row 1 (RS): (P1, K1) twice, P4, (K2, P2) 5 times, K2, P4, (K1, P1) twice.

Row 2: (K1, P1) twice, K4, P2, (K2, P2) 5 times, K4, (P1, K1) twice.

The last 2 rows sets the rib patt, rep the last 2 rows once more then row 1 again.

Row 6 (WS): (K1, P1) twice, K4, (P1, m1, P1, K1, m1, K1, P2, K1, m1, K1, P1, m1, P1, K2) twice, K2, (P1, K1) twice. *46 sts.*

CABLE STRIP 1

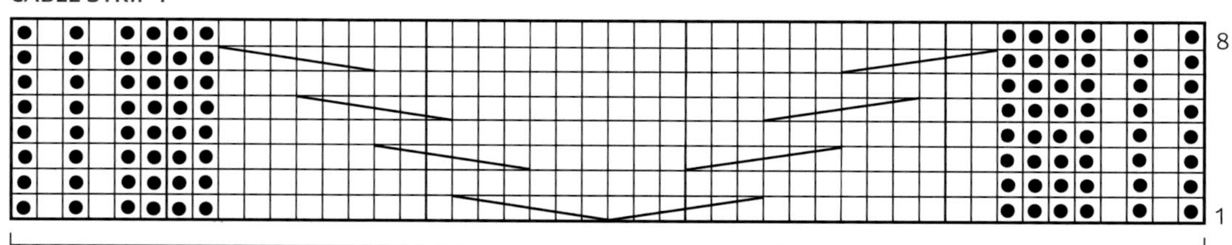

CABLE STRIP 2

6

1

46 sts

KEY

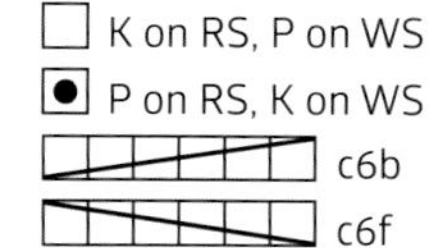

Cont to work from Chart, beg at bottom right hand corner [1st row is RS of work].

Work the 6-row patt rep 51 times, then rows 1 to 5 once ending with WS facing for next row.

311 rows of chart worked.

Next row (WS): (K1, P1) twice, K4, (p2tog, P1) twice, P2, (p2tog, P1) twice, K2, (P1, P2tog) twice, P2, (P1, P2tog) twice, K4, (P1, K1) twice.

38 sts.

Work the rib patt as set for 6 rows ending with RS facing for next row.

Bind off in rib.

FINISHING

Mattress stitch or slip stich the 3 strips neatly together with strip 1 at center.

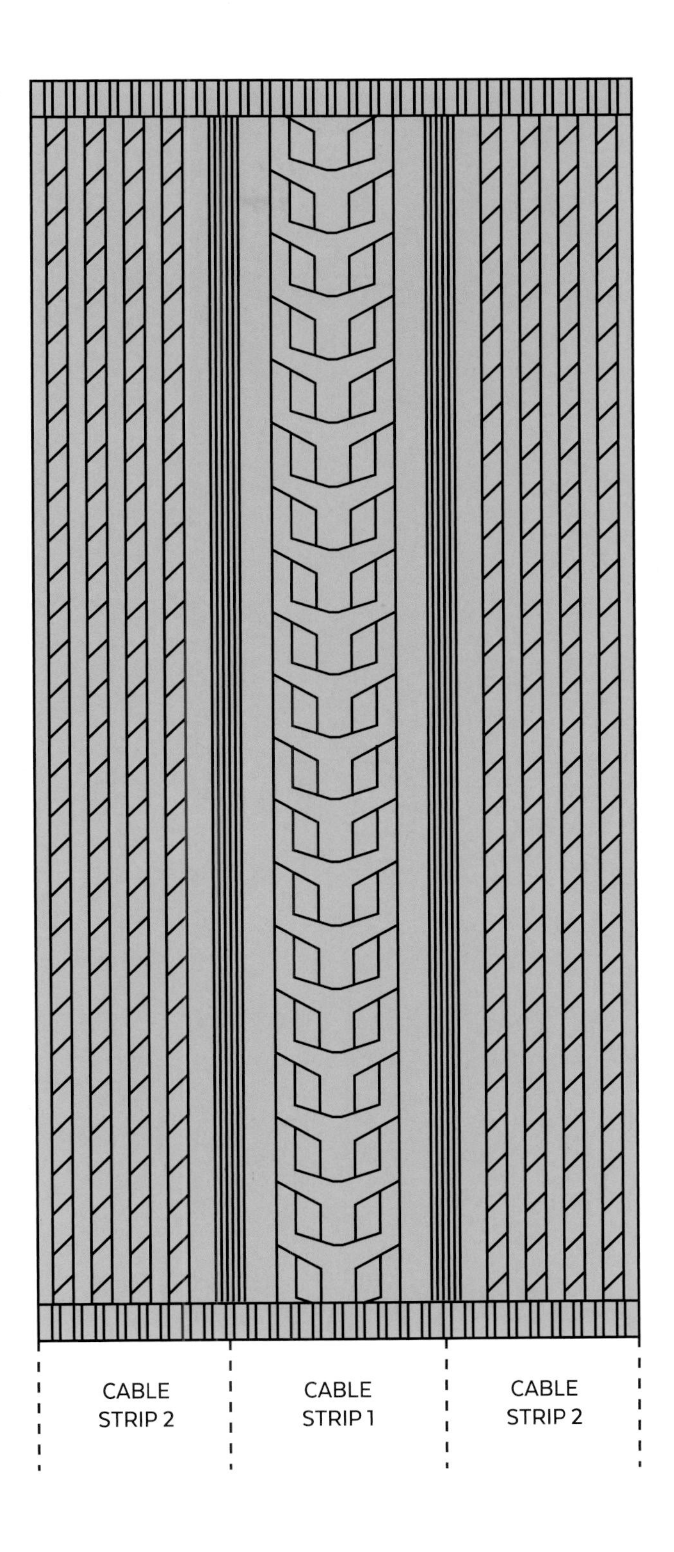

winter trees pillow

YARN

Alpaca Color

Marble	145	6 x 1¾oz/131yd
OR		
Felted Tweed		
Stone	190	6 x 1¾oz/191yd
OR		
Pure Wool DK		
Flint	105	6 x 1¾oz/142yd

NEEDLES

1 pair US 6 (4 mm) needles.

EXTRAS

19½ in (50 cm) square pillow form
90 x Debbie Abrahams size 6 beads

GAUGE

22 sts and 30 rows to 4 in (10cm) square measured over stockinette stitch using US 6 (4 mm) needles, or size required to obtain correct gauge.

FINISHED SIZE

Pillow measures approx 19½ in x19½ in (50 cm x 50 cm)

ABBREVIATIONS

See page 93.

Special Note for Beads

Place bead (on WS); place bead by taking yarn to RS of work, slipping bead up next to the stitch just worked, slip next stitch purlways from left needle to right needle and bring yarn back to WS, leaving bead sitting in front of slipped stitch.

NOTE

When working from Chart, right side rows are read from right to left; wrong side rows are read from left to right.

PILLOW FRONT

LACE TREE BLOCK 1 [make 5]

Cast on 37 sts using US 6 (4 mm) needles.
Cont to work from chart, beg at bottom right hand corner (1st row is RS of work) until all 53 rows have been worked, ending with WS facing for next row.
Bind off knitwise.

TEXTURED TREE BLOCK 2 [make 4]

Cast on 37 sts using US 6 (4 mm) needles.
Cont to work from chart, beg at bottom right hand corner (1st row is RS of work) until all 53 rows have been worked, ending with WS facing for next row.
Bind off knitwise

PILLOW BACK

Cast on 111 sts using US 6 (4 mm) .
Beg with a knit row, cont to work in stockinette stitch throughout until work measures 19½ in (50cm) from cast on edge, ending with RS facing for next row.
Bind off.

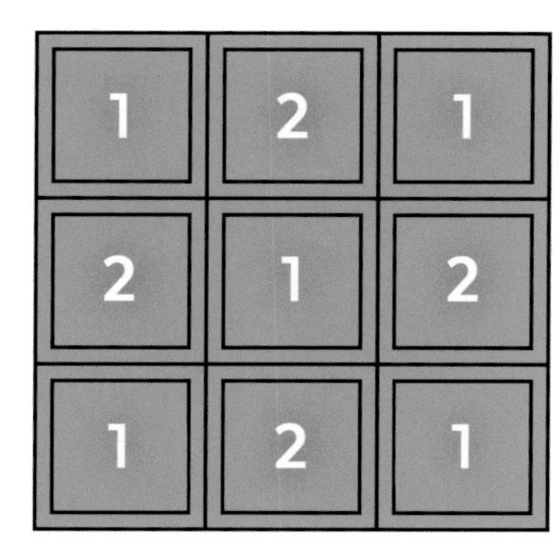

FINISHING

To form Pillow front: Join blocks as shown in diagram to form a square 3 squares wide and 3 squares long [9 blocks in total] with the "Lace Tree" block in each corner and at center.

Join both sides of pillow together using back stitch (or mattress stitch if preferred) along 3 sides. Insert pillow form, then close 4th side.

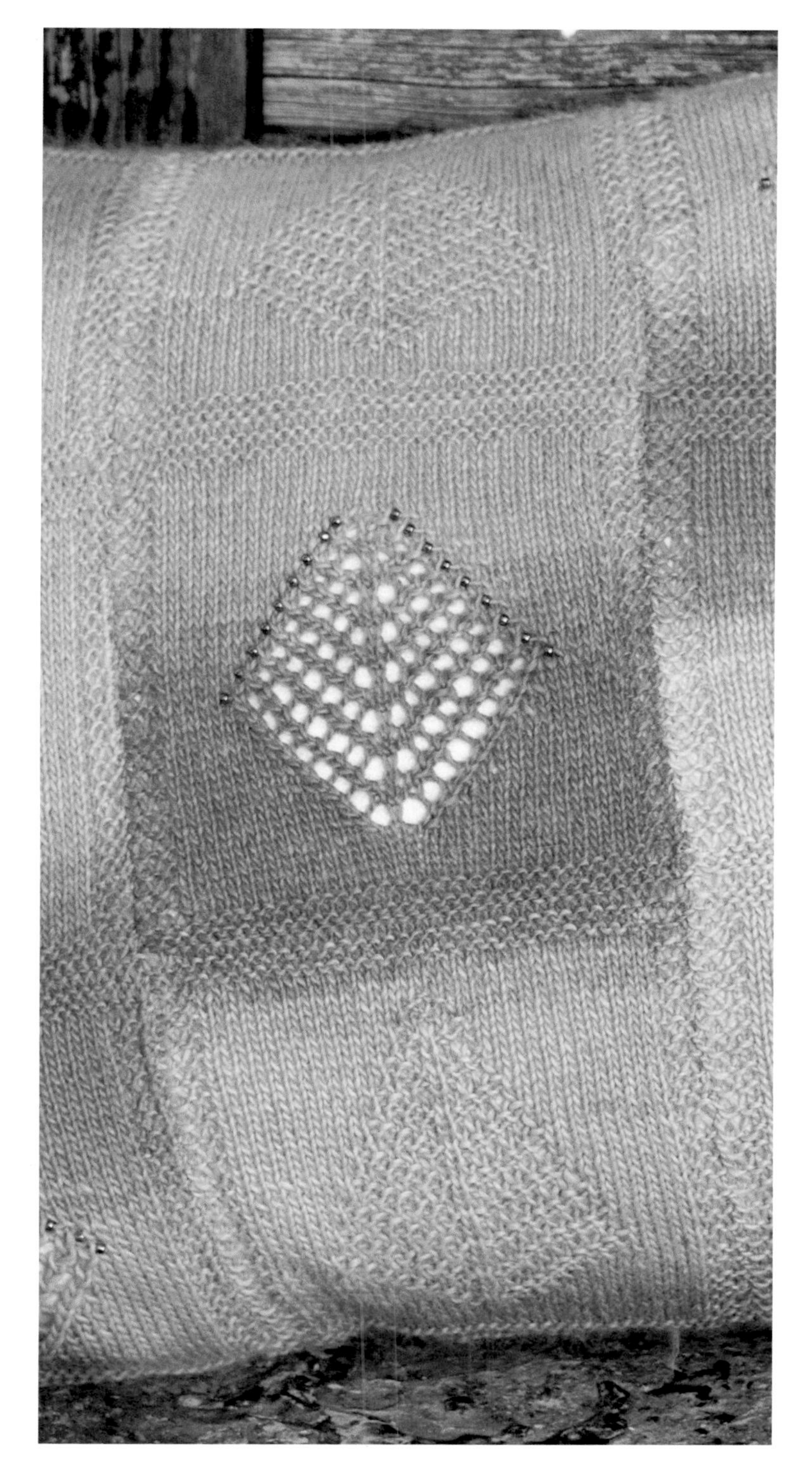

LACE TREE BLOCK 1

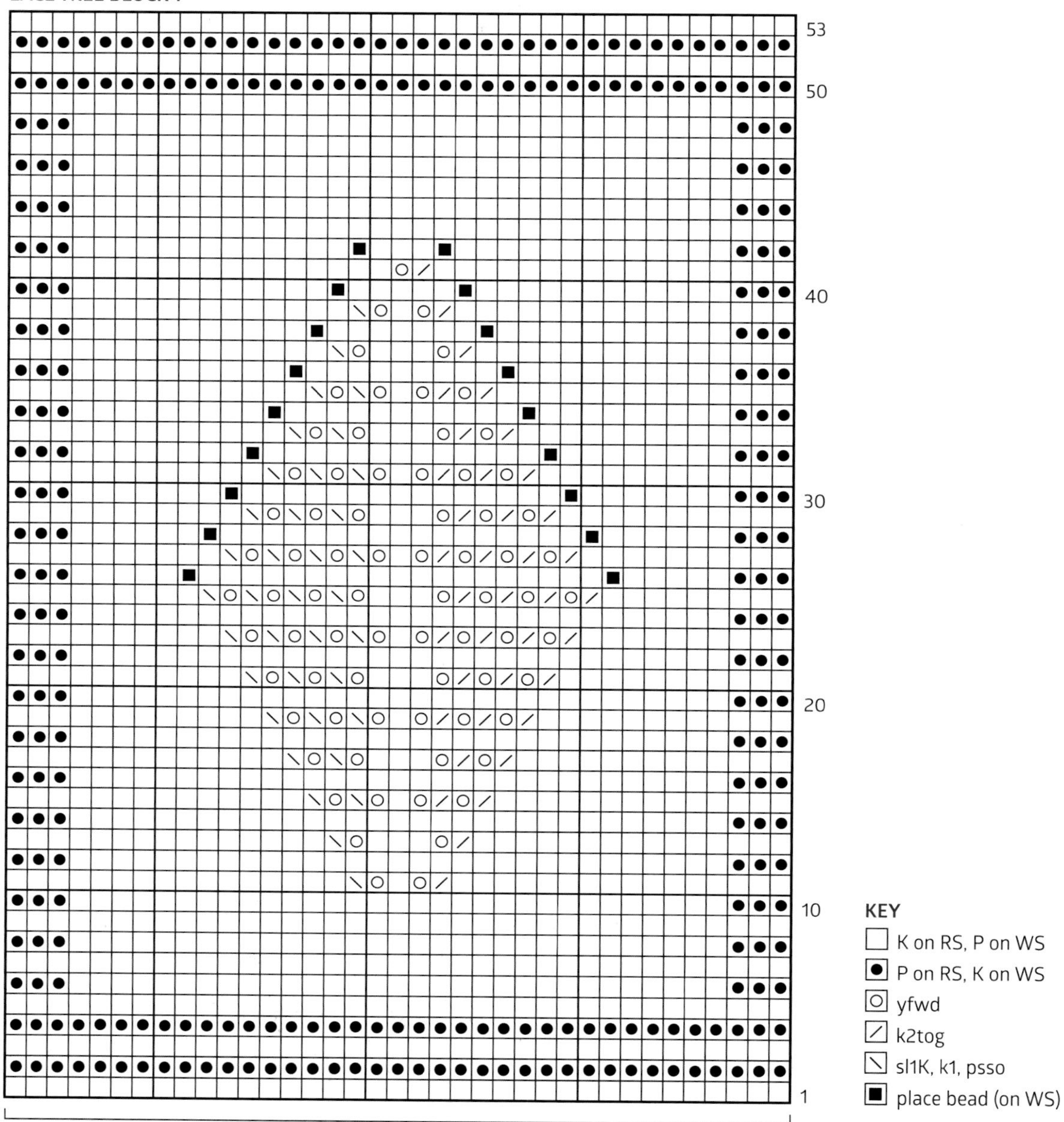

TEXTURED TREE BLOCK 2

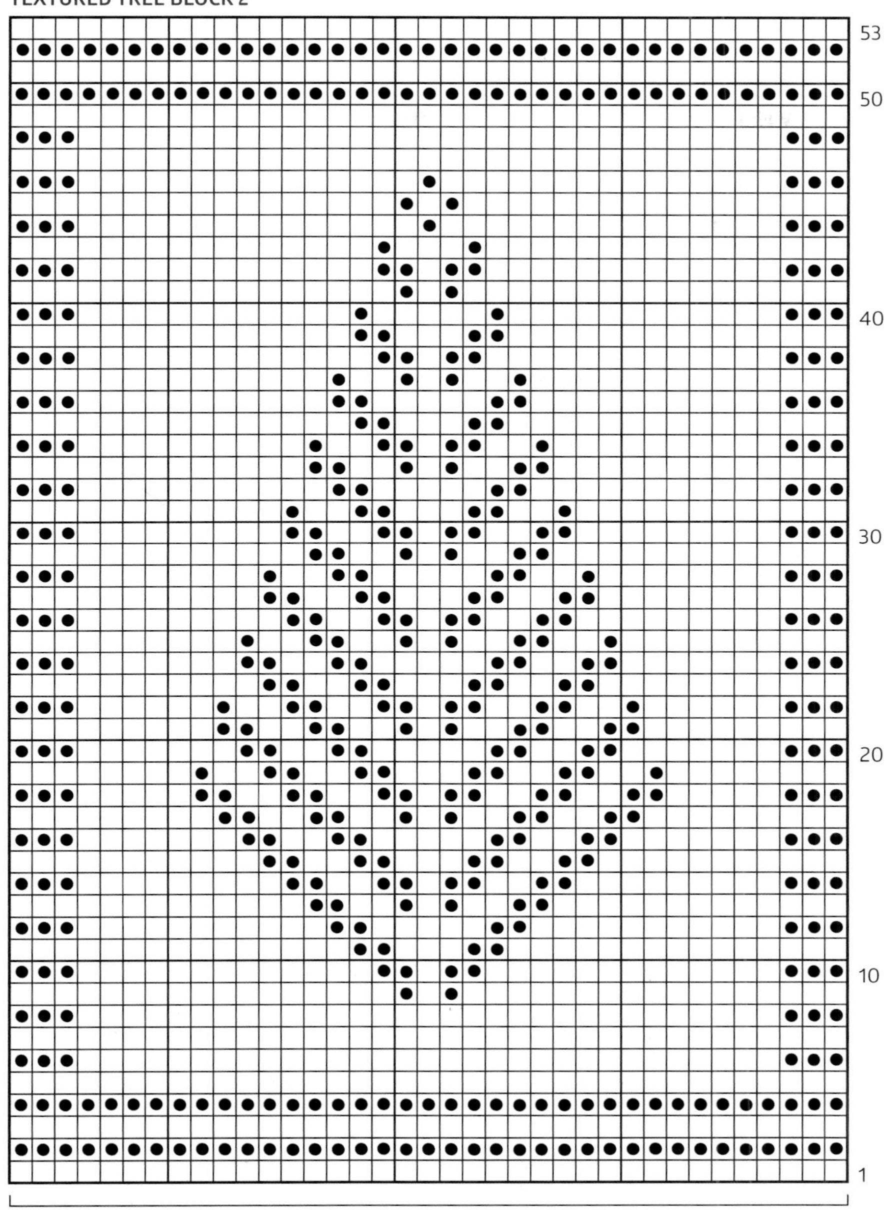

little folk pillow

YARN

Wool Cotton 4 ply

A	Cloudy	505	3 x 1¾oz/197yd
B	Misty	496	2 x 1¾oz/197yd

OR

Summerlite 4 ply

A	Washed Linen	418	3 x 1¾oz/191yd
B	Pepper Pot	431	2 x 1¾oz/191yd

NEEDLES

1 pair US 3 (3.25 mm) [US2/3 (3 mm) if using Summerlite 4ply] needles.
1 x US 2 (2.75 mm) long circular needle.

EXTRAS

Pillow form 14 in (35 cm) square.
Backing fabric 15½ in (39cm) square.

GAUGE

28 sts and 36 rows to 4in (10 mm) square measured over stockinette stitch using US 3 (3.25 mm) [US2/3 (3 mm) if using Summerlite 4ply] needles, or size required to obtain correct gauge.

FINISHED SIZE

Pillow measures approx 14 in (35 cm) x 14 in (35 cm)

ABBREVIATIONS

M1 = make one stitch by inserting needle from behind under the running thread (which is the strand running from the base of the stitch just worked to the base of the next stitch) and lift this thread onto left hand needle; then knit one stitch in to the back of it.
See also page 93.

NOTE

When working from Charts, right side rows are read from right to left; wrong side rows are read from left to right.

PILLOW FRONT

BLOCKS (make 1 of each of the 9 blocks)

Cast on 29 sts using US 3 (3.25 mm) [US 2/3 (3 mm) if using Summerlite 4ply] needles and yarn A for blocks 1, 3, 5, 7 and 9 and yarn B for blocks 2, 4, 6 and 8.

Beg with a K row cont to work each chart entirely in stockinette stitch using the Fair Isle technique beg at bottom right hand corner (1st row is RS of work) until all 38 rows have been worked, ending with RS facing for next row.

Bind off.

FINISHING

Using back stitch or mattress stitch if preferred, join all 9 blocks as shown by diagram, to form a square 3 blocks wide and 3 blocks long.

Trim backing fabric to same size as knitted front adding seam allowance along all edges. Fold seam allowances to WS along all edges of backing fabric.

Lay backing fabric on to knitted piece with WS facing and sew in place along 3 sides. Insert pillow form, then close 4th side.

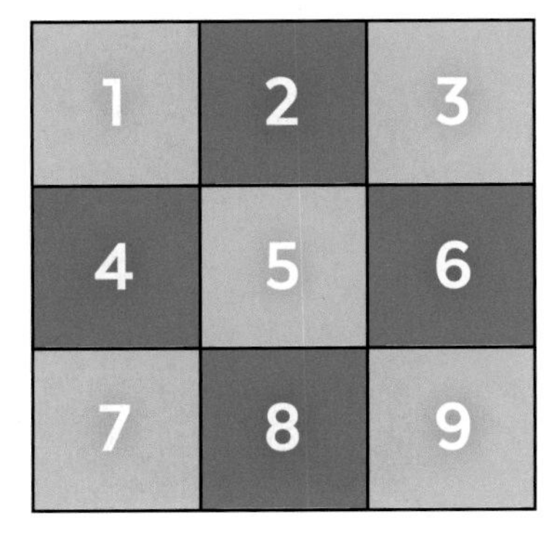

KEY

Color A

Color B

BLOCK 1

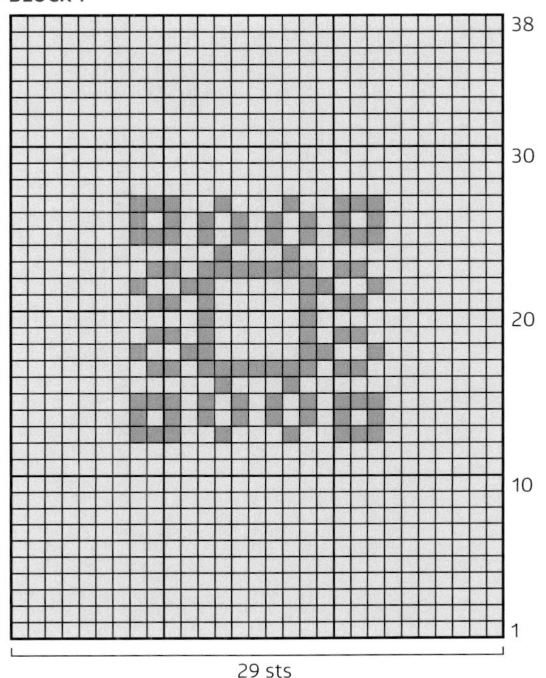

BLOCK 2

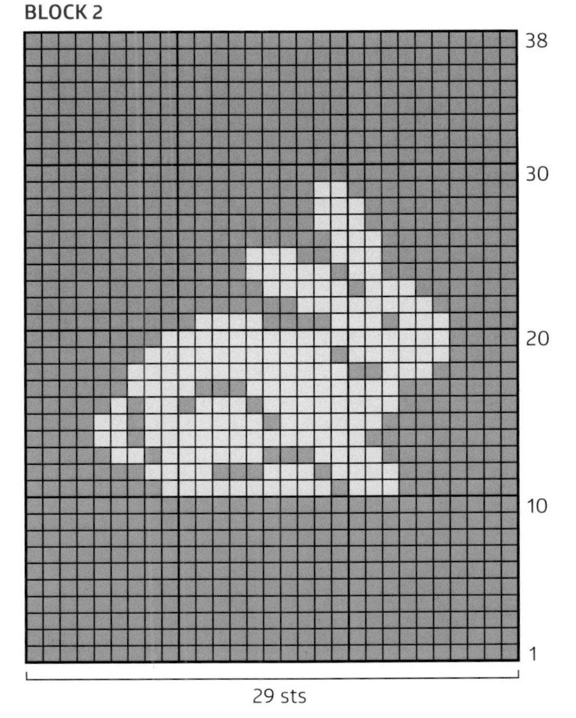

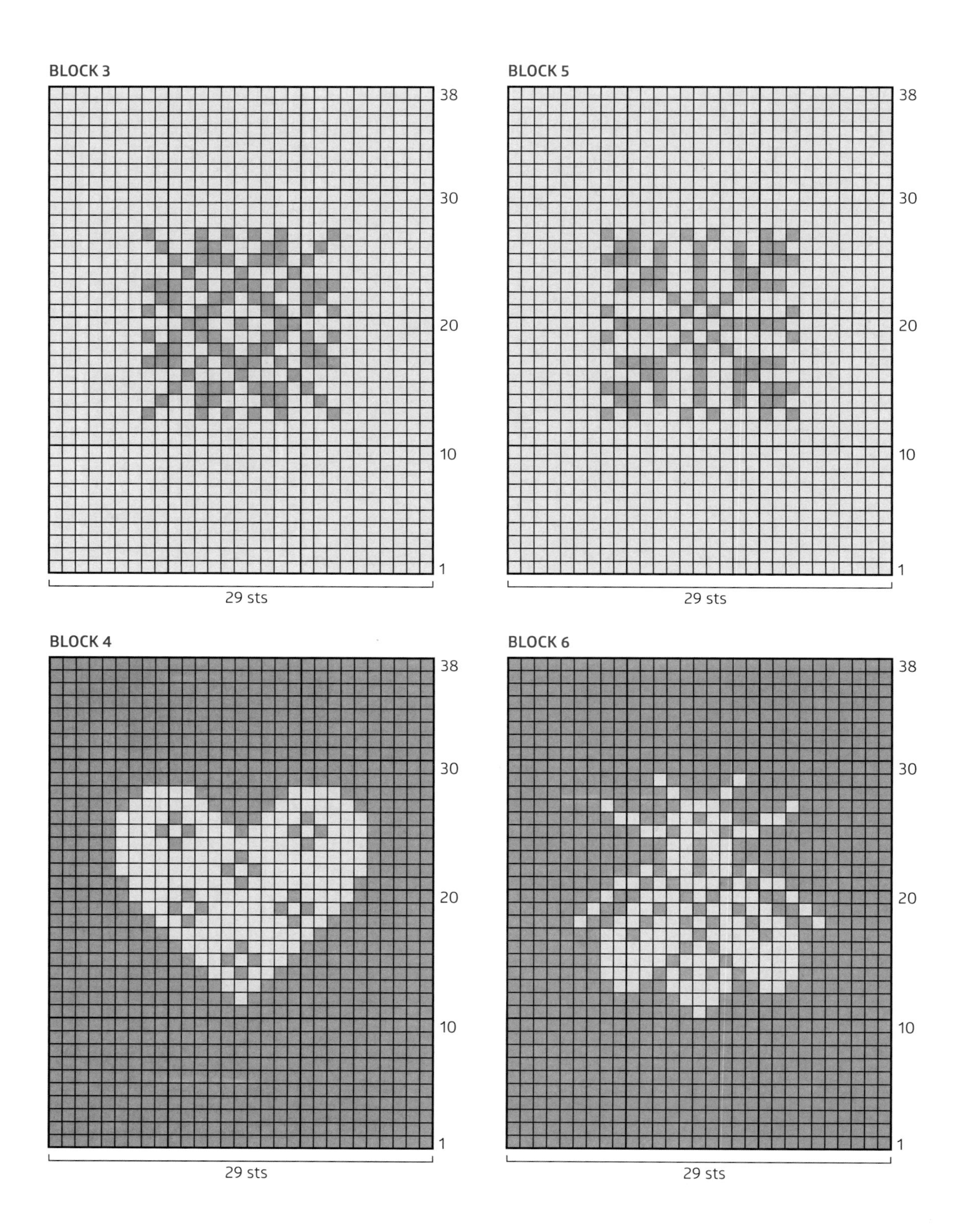

BLOCK 3
38
30
20
10
1
29 sts
BLOCK 5
38
30
20
10
1
29 sts
BLOCK 4
38
30
20
10
1
29 sts
BLOCK 6
38
30
20
10
1
29 sts

BLOCK 7

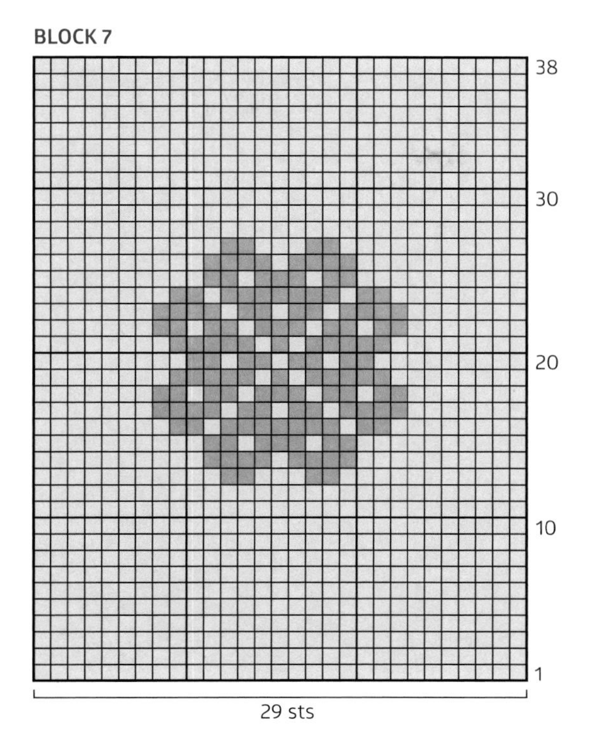

BLOCK 9

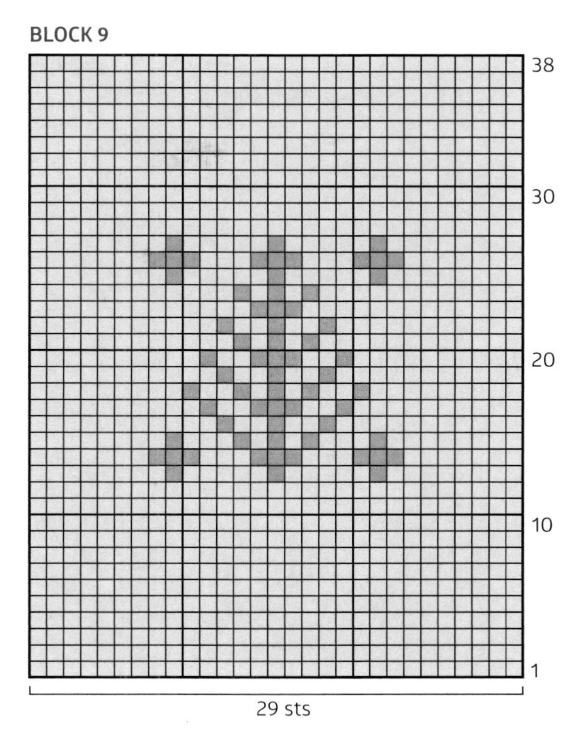

BLOCK 8

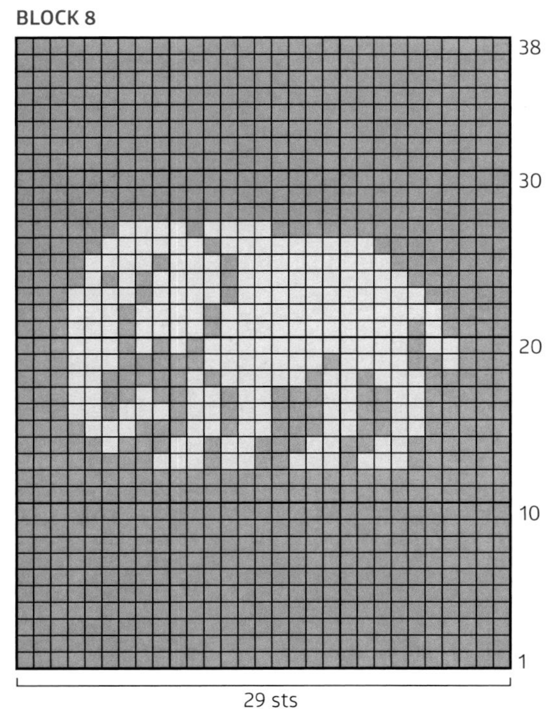

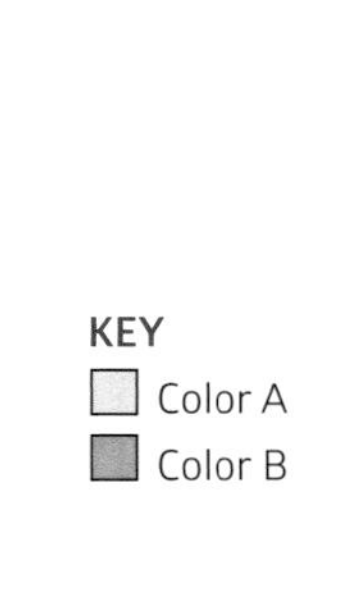

little folk blanket

YARN

Wool Cotton 4 ply

A	Cloudy	505	3 x 1¾oz/197yd
B	Misty	496	2 x 1¾oz/197yd
C	Prune	506	1 x 1¾oz/197yd

OR

Summerlite 4 ply

A	Washed Linen	418	3 x 1¾oz/191yd
B	Pepper Pot	431	2 x 1¾oz/191yd
C	Aubergine	432	1 x 1¾oz/191yd

NEEDLES

1 pair US 3 (3.25 mm) [US2/3 (3 mm) if using Summerlite 4ply] needles.
1 x US 2 (2.75 mm) long circular needle.

GAUGE

28 sts and 36 rows to 4 in (10 cm) square measured over stockinette stitch using US 3 (3.25 mm) [US2/3 (3 mm) if using Summerlite 4ply] needles, or size required to obtain correct gauge.

FINISHED SIZE

Crib blanket measures approx 23½ in (60 cm) x 32½ in (83 cm)

ABBREVIATIONS

M1 = make one stitch by inserting needle from behind under the running thread (which is the strand running from the base of the stitch just worked to the base of the next stitch) and lift this thread onto left hand needle; then knit one stitch in to the back of it.
See also page 93.

NOTE

When working from Charts, right side rows are read from right to left; wrong side rows are read from left to right.

CRIB BLANKET

BLOCK 1 (make 4)

Cast on 29 sts using US 3 (3.25 mm) [US2/3 (3 mm) if using Summerlite 4ply] needles and yarn A.
Beg with a K row cont to work Chart (see page 67) entirely in stockinette stitch using the Fair Isle technique beg at bottom right hand corner (1st row is RS of work) until all 38 rows have been worked, ending with RS facing for next row.
Cast off.

BLOCKS 2-9

Work the following Blocks as set by Block 1 from the relevant charts on pages 67-69, casting on using yarn A for blocks 3, 5, 7 and 9 and yarn B for blocks 2, 4, 6 and 8;
Block 2 [make 4]
Block 3 [make 2]
Block 4 [make 6]
Block 5 [make 6]
Block 6 [make 3]
Block 7 [make 4]
Block 8 [make 4]
Block 9 [make 2]
Total = 35 Blocks

FINISHING

Using back stitch or mattress stitch if preferred, join all 35 blocks as shown by diagram opposite, to form a large rectangle 5 blocks wide and 7 blocks long.

1	2	3	2	1
4	5	6	5	4
7	8	9	8	7
4	5	6	5	4
1	2	3	2	1
4	5	6	5	4
7	8	9	8	7

TOP EDGING

With RS facing using US 2 (2.75 mm) long circular needle and yarn C pick up and K 180 sts evenly along bound-off edge of blanket.

Row 1 (WS): Knit.

Row 2: K1, m1, K to last st, m1, K1.

Rep the last 2 rows twice more. *186 sts.*

Bind off knitwise.

BOTTOM EDGING

With RS facing US 2 (2.75 mm) long circular needle and yarn C pick up and K 180 sts evenly along cast-on edge of blanket.

Row 1 (WS): Knit.

Row 2: K1, m1, K to last st, m1, K1.

Rep the last 2 rows twice more. *186 sts.*

Bind off knitwise.

SIDE EDGINGS [both alike]

With RS facing using US 2 (2.75 mm) long circular needle and yarn C pick up and K 250 sts evenly along cast-on edge of blanket.

Row 1 (WS): Knit.

Row 2: K1, m1, K to last st, m1, K1.

Rep the last 2 rows twice more. *256 sts.*

Cast off knitwise.

Join corners of all edgings.

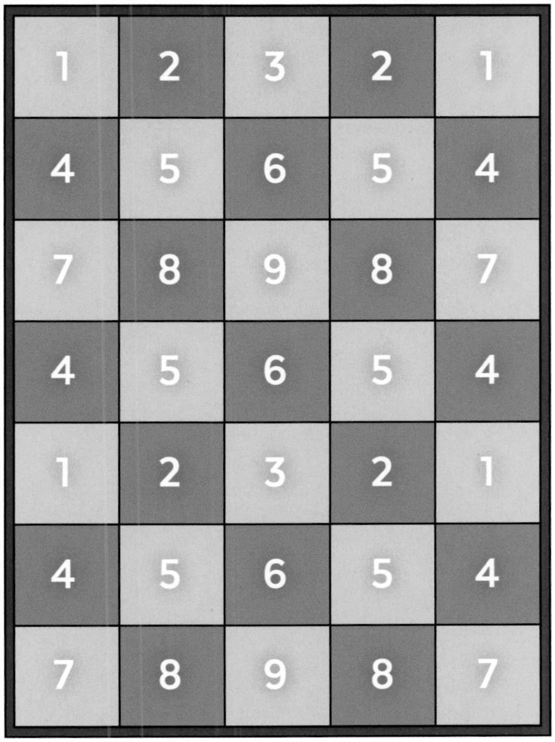

modern art blanket

YARN

Pure Wool Superwash Worsted

A	Mustard	131	3 x 3½oz/219yd
B	Umber	110	2 x 3½oz/219yd
C	Oats	152	2 x 3½oz/219yd
D	Rosy	115	2 x 3½oz/219yd
E	Gold	133	1 x 3½oz/219yd
F	Granite	111	1 x 3½oz/219yd
G	Cocoa Bean	105	1 x 3½oz/219yd
OR			
A	Olive	125	3 x 3½oz/219yd
B	Damson	150	2 x 3½oz/219yd
C	Mole	157	2 x 3½oz/219yd
D	Rust	106	2 x 3½oz/219yd
E	Gold	133	1 x 3½oz/219yd
F	Granite	111	1 x 3½oz/219yd
G	Hawthorn	141	1 x 3½oz/219yd
OR **(Monochrome Colorway)**			
A	Moonstone	112	3 x 13½oz/219yd
B	Black	109	2 x 3½oz/219yd
C/G	Mole	157	3 x 3½oz/219yd
D	Charcoal Grey	155	2 x 3½oz/219yd
E	Almond	103	1 x 3½oz/219yd
F	Granite	111	1 x 3½oz/219yd

NEEDLES

1 pair US 6 (4 mm) needles.

GAUGE

20 sts and 34 rows to 4in (10cm) square measured over garter stitch using US 6 (4 mm) needles, or required size to obtain correct gauge.

FINISHED SIZE

Blanket measures approx 38½ in (97.5 cm) x 47 in (120 cm)

ABBREVIATIONS

See page 93.

BLANKET

STRIP 1

Cast on 39 sts using US 6 (4 mm) needles and yarn A.
Cont in garter stitch as folls [ie. every row K]:-
190 rows using yarn A.
76 rows using yarn B.
189 rows using yarn C, ending with WS facing for next row.
Bind off knitwise [on WS].

STRIP 2

Cast on 39 sts using US 6 (4 mm) needles and yarn D.
Cont in garter stitch as folls [ie. every row K]:-
228 rows using yarn D.
38 rows using yarn E.
189 rows using yarn D, ending with WS facing for next row.
Bind off knitwise [on WS].

STRIP 3

Cast on 39 sts using US 6 (4 mm) needles and yarn F.
Cont in garter stitch as folls [ie. every row K]:-
152 rows using yarn F.
76 rows using yarn A.
38 rows using yarn G.
189 rows using yarn A, ending with WS facing for next row.
Bind off knitwise [on WS].

STRIP 4

Cast on 39 sts using US 6 (4 mm) needles and yarn B.

Cont in garter stitch as folls [ie. every row K]:-

Work 455 rows using yarn B, ending with WS facing for next row.

Bind off knitwise [on WS].

STRIP 5

Cast on 39 sts using US 6 (4 mm) needles and yarn A.

Cont in garter stitch as folls [ie. every row K]:-

190 rows using yarn A.

76 rows using yarn F.

189 rows using yarn C, ending with WS facing for next row.

Bind off knitwise [on WS].

FINISHING

Matching the garter ridge-rows of each strip and using a neat mattress stitch to join strips together, join all 5 strips together as shown in diagram.

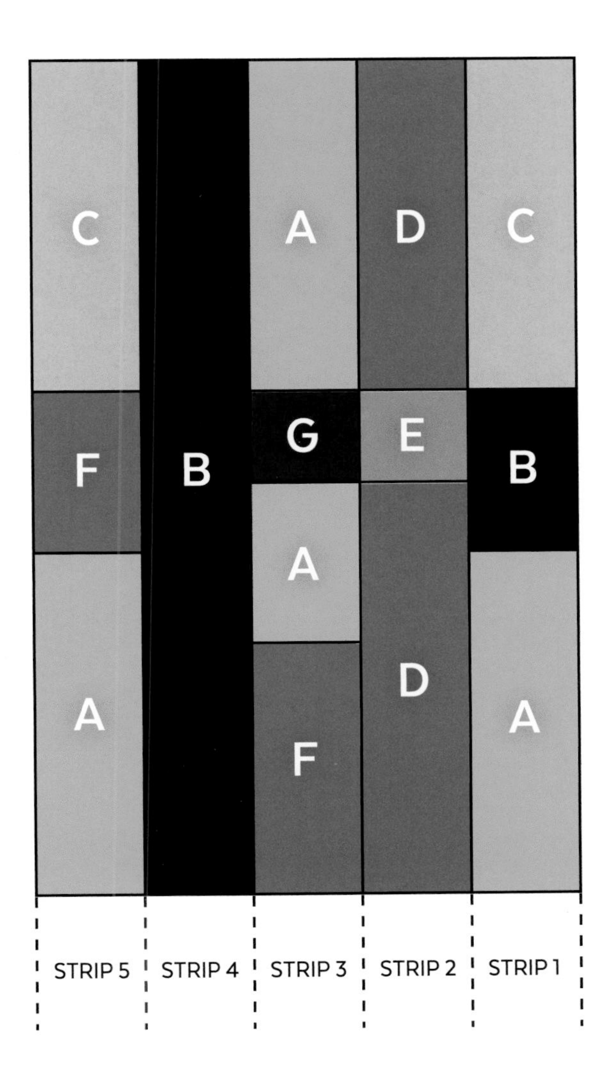

icelandic pillow

YARN

Felted Tweed Aran

A	Stoney	742	2 x 1¾oz/87yd
B	Mahogany	734	2 x 1¾oz/87yd

OR

Felted Tweed Aran

A	Scree	756	2 x 1¾oz/87yd
B	Carbon	759	2 x 1¾oz/87yd

NEEDLES

1 pair US 7 (4.5 mm) needles.

EXTRAS

19½ in (50 cm) square pillow form

21½ in (54 cm) square of backing fabric

GAUGE

16 sts and 23 rows to 4 in (10 cm) square measured over stockinette stitch using US 7 (4.5 mm) needles, or size required to obtain correct gauge.

FINISHED SIZE

Pillow measures approx 19½ in x19½ in (50 cm x 50 cm).

ABBREVIATIONS

See page 93.

NOTE

When working from Charts, right side rows are read from right to left; wrong side rows are read from left to right.

PILLOW FRONT

BLOCK 1 (make 5)

Cast on 31 sts using US 7 (4.5 mm) needles and yarn B.
Cont to work from Chart beg at bottom right hand corner (1st row is RS of work), working in st st throughout and using the Fairisle technique until all 31 rows have been worked, ending with WS facing for next row.
Bind off knitwise.

BLOCK 2 (make 2)

Cast on 31 sts using US 7 (4.5 mm) needles and yarn A.
Work as Block 1.

BLOCK 3 (make 2)

Cast on 31 sts using US 7 (4.5 mm) needles and yarn A.
Work as Block 1.

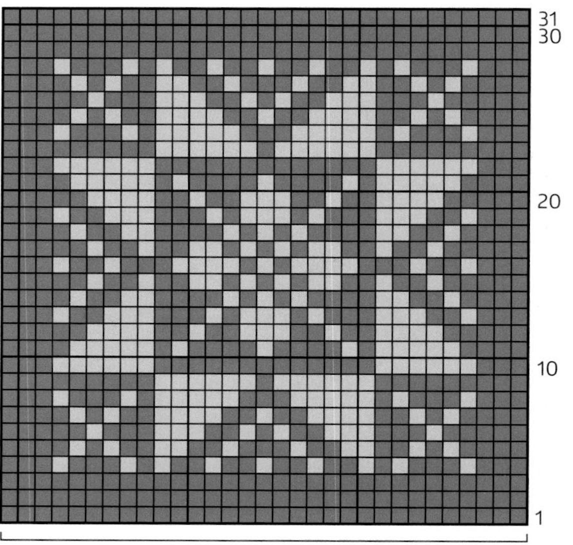

FINISHING

To form Pillow front: Join blocks as shown on diagram, to form a square 3 blocks wide and 3 blocks long [9 blocks in total].

Trim backing fabric to same size as knitted section, adding seam allowance along all edges. Fold seam allowance to WS along all edges of backing fabric. Lay backing fabric onto knitted piece with WS facing and sew backing fabric in place along 3 sides. Insert pillow form, then close 4th side.

1	2	1
3	1	3
1	2	1

KEY

Color A

Color B

BLOCK 2

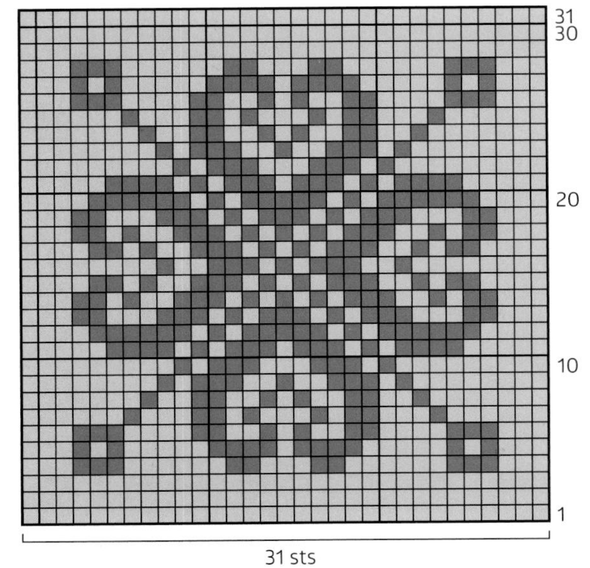

BLOCK 3

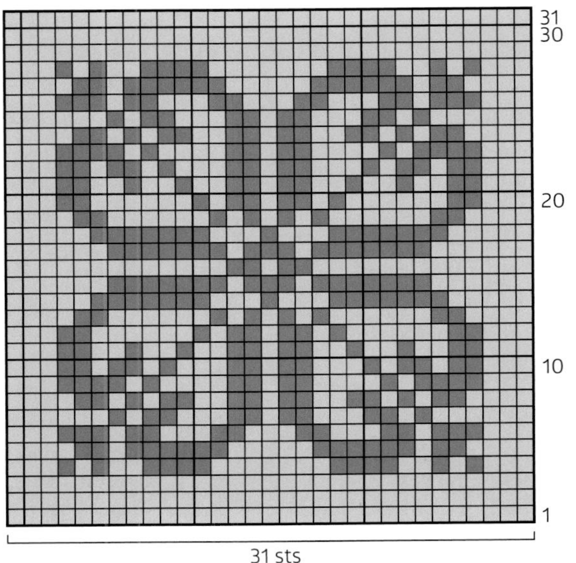

springtime blanket

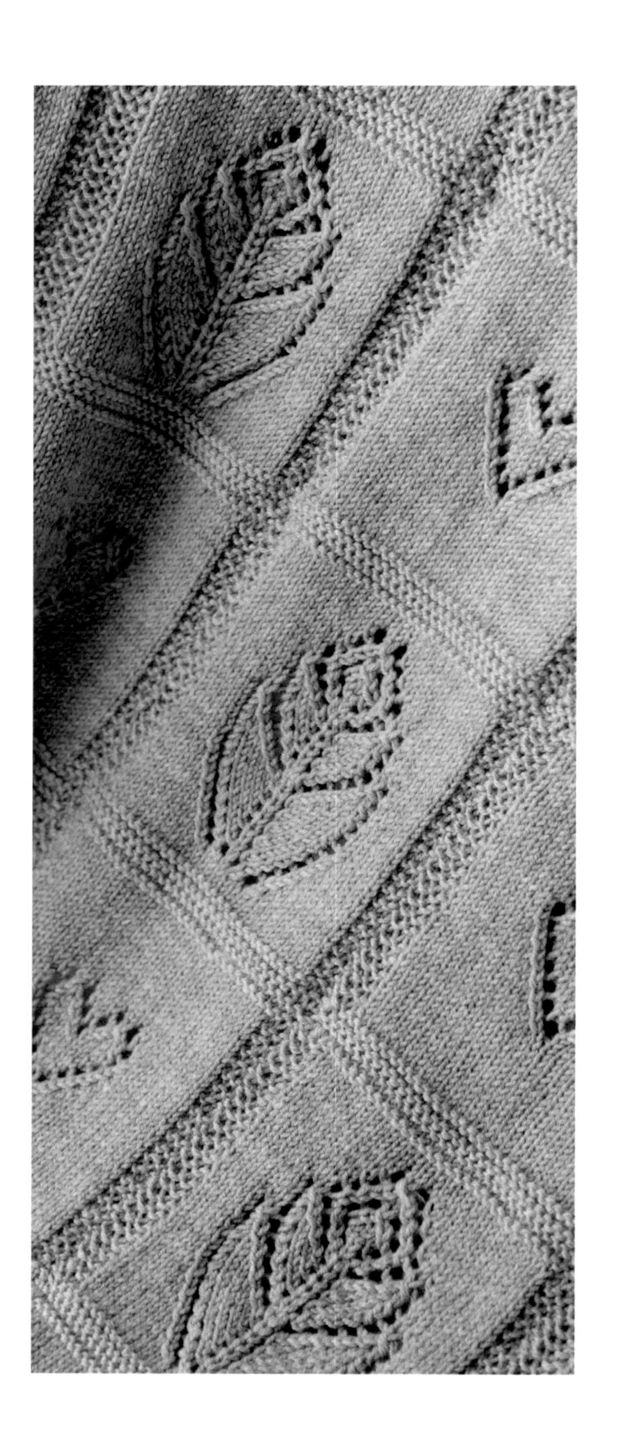

YARN

Superfine Merino 4 ply

Marble	269	1¾oz/181yd

NEEDLES

1 pair US 3 (3.25 mm) needles.

GAUGE

28 sts and 36 rows to 4 in (10 cm) square measured over stocking stitch using US 3 (3.25 mm) needles, or size required to obtain correct gauge.

FINISHED SIZE

Blanket measures approx 34½ in (87 cm) x 44 in (112 cm).

ABBREVIATIONS

See page 93.

NOTE

When working from Charts, right side rows are read from right to left; wrong side rows are read from left to right.

BLANKET

BLOCK 1 [make 32]

Cast on 33 sts using US 3 (3.25 mm) needles.

Cont to work from Chart on page 78 beg at bottom right hand corner (1st row is RS of work) until all 49 rows have been worked, ending with WS facing for next row.

Cast off knitwise.

BLOCK 2 [make 31]

Cast on 33 sts using US 3 (3.25 mm) needles.

Cont to work from Chart on page 79 beg at bottom right hand corner (1st row is RS of work) until all 49 rows have been worked, ending with WS facing for next row.

Bind off knitwise.

FINISHING

Using back stitch or mattress stitch if preferred, join all 63 squares as shown by diagram, to form a large rectangle 7 blocks wide and 9 blocks long.

1	2	1	2	1	2	1
2	1	2	1	2	1	2
1	2	1	2	1	2	1
2	1	2	1	2	1	2
1	2	1	2	1	2	1
2	1	2	1	2	1	2
1	2	1	2	1	2	1
2	1	2	1	2	1	2
1	2	1	2	1	2	1

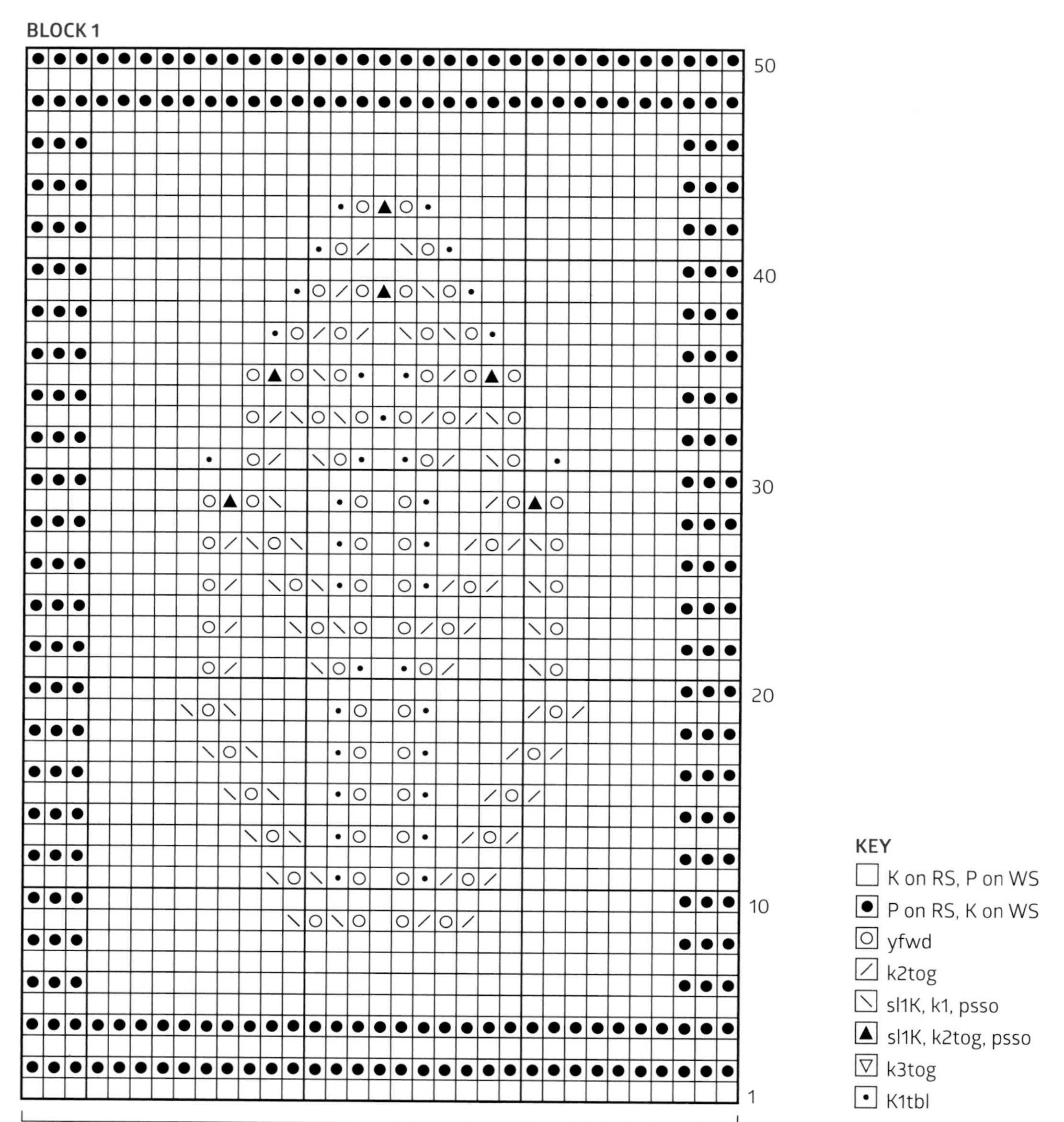
BLOCK 1
50
40
30
20
10
1
33 sts
KEY
K on RS, P on WS
P on RS, K on WS
yfwd
k2tog
sl1K, k1, psso
sl1K, k2tog, psso
k3tog
K1tbl

BLOCK 2

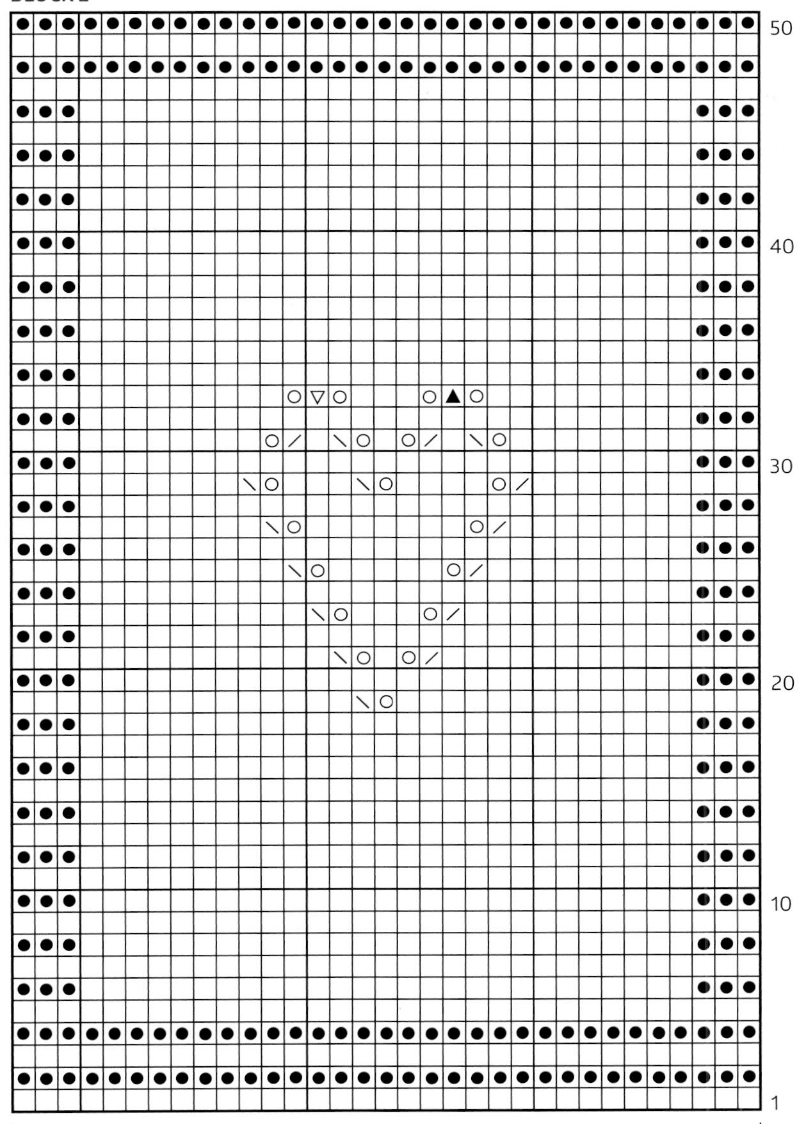

springtime pillow

YARN
Summerlite 4 ply

Washed Linen	418	3 x 1¾oz/191yd

NEEDLES
1 pair US 2/3 (3mm) needles.

EXTRAS
Pillow form 35 cm (14 in) square.

GAUGE
28 sts and 36 rows to 4 in (10 cm) square measured over stockinette stitch using US 2/3 (3mm) needles, or size required to obtain correct gauge.

FINISHED SIZE
Pillow measures approx 14 in (35 cm) x 14 in (35 cm)

ABBREVIATIONS
See page 93.

NOTE
When working from Charts, right side rows are read from right to left; wrong side rows are read from left to right.

PILLOW FRONT
BLOCK 1 [make 5]

Cast on 33 sts using US 2/3 (3mm)) needles.

Cont to work from Chart on page 78 beg at bottom right hand corner (1st row is RS of work) until all 49 rows have been worked, ending with WS facing for next row.

Bind off knitwise.

BLOCK 2 [make 4]

Cast on 33 sts using US 2/3 (3mm) needles.

Cont to work from Chart on page 79 beg at bottom right hand corner (1st row is RS of work) until all 49 rows have been worked, ending with WS facing for next row.

Bind off knitwise.

PILLOW BACK
Cast on 99 sts using US 2/3 (3mm) needles.

Beg with a knit row cont in stockinette stitch until work measures 14 in (35 cm), ending with RS facing for next row.

Bind off.

FINISHING
To form Pillow front Join blocks as shown on photograph to form a square 3 blocks wide and 3 blocks long [9 blocks in total] with block 1 in each corner and at center.

Join both sides of pillow together using back stitch or mattress stitch if preferred, along 3 sides. Insert pillow form, then close 4th side.

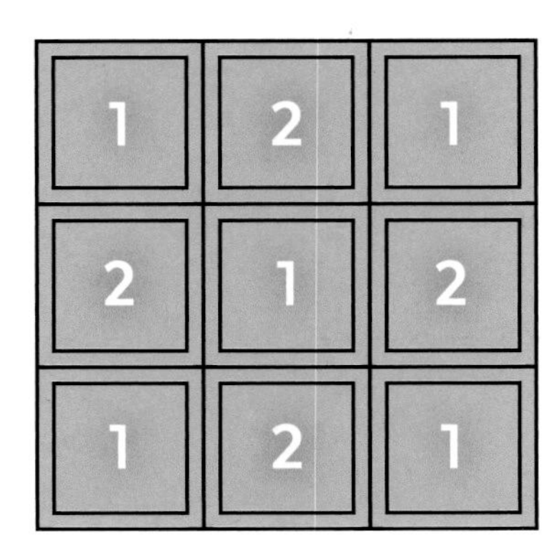

beach stripes blanket

YARN

Wool Cotton

A	Rich	911	2 x 1¾oz/124yd
B	Moss Gray	990	2 x 1¾oz/124yd
C	Elf	946	2 x 1¾oz/124yd
D	Lichen	922	2 x 1¾oz/124yd
E	Antique	900	2 x 1¾oz/124yd
F	Larkspur	988	2 x 1¾oz/124yd
G	Misty	903	1 x 1¾oz/124yd
H	Inky	908	2 x 1¾oz/124yd
I	Pier	983	1 x 1¾oz/124yd

OR

Handknit Cotton

A	Rosso	215	2 x 1¾oz/148yd
B	Linen	205	2 x 1¾oz/148yd
C	Gooseberry	219	2 x 1¾oz/148yd
D	Forest	370	2 x 1¾oz/148yd
E	Ecru	251	2 x 1¾oz/148yd
F	Thunder	335	2 x 1¾oz/148yd
G	Slate	347	1 x 1¾oz/148yd
H	Black	252	2 x 1¾oz/148yd
I	Atlantic	346	1 x 1¾oz/148yd

NEEDLES

1 pair US 3 (3.25 mm) needles

1 x US 3 (3.25 mm) long circular needle

GAUGE

23 sts and 46 rows to 4 in (10 cm) square measured over garter stitch using US 3 (3.25 mm) needles, or required size to obtain correct gauge

.

FINISHED SIZE

Blanket measures approx 27½ in (70 cm) x 145½ in (116 cm)

ABBREVIATIONS

See page 93.

BLANKET

STRIP 1 [make 2]

Cast on 31 sts using US 3 (3.25 mm) needles and yarn A.

Cont in garter stitch as folls [ie. every row K]:-

Work 4 rows using yarn A [for lower border]

Cont in garter stitch work the following stripe sequence 5 times:-

18 rows using yarn B.

6 rows using yarn C.

6 rows using yarn D.

18 rows using yarn E.

6 rows using yarn C.

18 rows using yarn D.

6 rows using yarn B.

18 rows using yarn C.

6 rows using yarn A.

510 rows of stripe sequence worked.

Knit 18 rows using yarn B.

Knit 5 rows using yarn A, WS facing for next row:-

Next row (WS): Using yarn A bind off knitwise [on WS - the last 6 rows form top border].

STRIP 2 [make 2]

Cast on 31 sts using US 3 (3.25 mm) needles and yarn A.

Cont in garter stitch as folls [ie. every row K]:-

Work 4 rows using yarn A [for lower border].

Cont in garter stitch work the following stripe sequence 5 times:

18 rows using yarn F.

6 rows using yarn G.

6 rows using yarn H.

6 rows using yarn E.
6 rows using yarn H.
18 rows using yarn I.
6 rows using yarn H.
6 rows using yarn C.
18 rows using yarn G.
6 rows using yarn E.
6 rows using yarn H.
510 rows of stripe sequence worked.
Knit 18 rows using yarn F.
Knit 5 rows using yarn A, WS facing for next row:-
Next row (WS): Using yarn A bind off knitwise [on WS - the last 6 rows form top border]

STRIP 3 [make 1]
Cast on 31 sts using US 3 (3.25 mm) needles and yarn A.
Cont in garter stitch as folls [ie. every row K]:
Work 4 rows using yarn A [for lower border].
Cont in garter stitch work the following stripe sequence 5 times:-
18 rows using yarn G.
6 rows using yarn H.
18 rows using yarn E.
6 rows using yarn G.
6 rows using yarn A.
6 rows using yarn G.
18 rows using yarn E.
6 rows using yarn H.
6 rows using yarn F.
6 rows using yarn H.
6 rows using yarn F.
510 rows of stripe sequence worked.
Knit 18 rows using yarn G.

Knit 5 rows using yarn A, WS facing for next row:

Next row (WS): Using yarn A bind off knitwise.

[on WS the last 6 rows form top border].

FINISHING

Matching the garter ridge rows of each strip and using a neat mattress stitch to join strips together, join all 5 strips as shown in illustration.

SIDE EDGINGS [both alike]

With RS facing using US 3 (3.25 mm) circular needle and yarn A, pick up and knit 265 sts along row end edge of blanket.

Knit 4 rows ending with WS facing for next row.

Next row (WS): Cast off knitwise

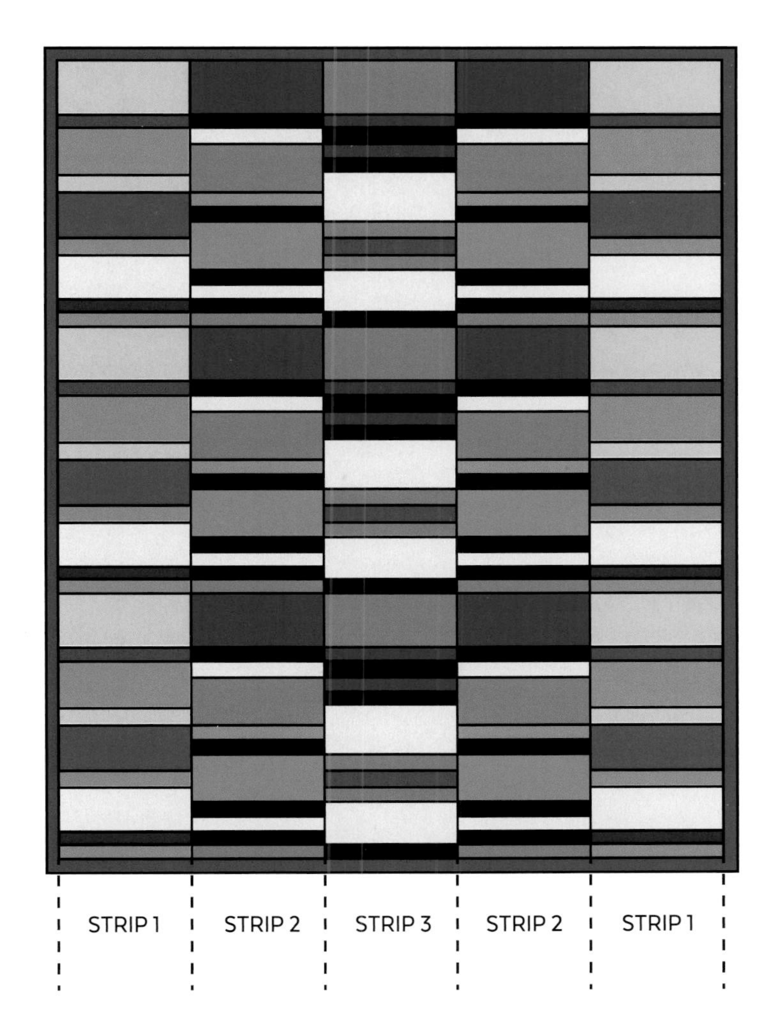

beach stripes mat

YARN

Wool Cotton

A	Rich	911	1 x 1¾oz/124yd ball
B	Moss Gray	990	1 x 1¾oz/124yd ball
C	Elf	946	1 x 1¾oz/124yd ball
D	Lichen	922	1 x 1¾oz/124yd ball
E	Antique	900	1 x 1¾oz/124yd ball
F	Larkspur	988	1 x 1¾oz/124yd ball
G	Misty	903	1 x 1¾oz/124yd ball
H	Inky	908	1 x 11¾oz/124yd ball
I	Pier	983	1 x 1¾oz/124yd ball

OR

Handknit Cotton

A	Rosso	215	1 x 1¾oz/148yd ball
B	Linen	205	1 x 1¾oz/148yd ball
C	Gooseberry	219	1 x 1¾oz/148yd ball
D	Forest	370	1 x 1¾oz/148yd ball
E	Ecru	251	1 x 1¾oz/148yd ball
F	Thunder	335	1 x 11¾oz/148yd ball
G	Slate	347	1 x 1¾oz/148yd ball
H	Black	252	1 x 1¾oz/148yd ball
I	Atlantic	346	1 x 1¾oz/148yd ball

NEEDLES

1 pair US 3 (3.25 mm) needles

GAUGE

23 sts and 46 rows to 4in (10 cm) square measured over garter stitch using US 3 (3.25 mm) needles, or required size to obtain correct gauge.

FINISHED SIZE

Mat measures approx 14 in (36 cm) x 11½ in (29 cm)

ABBREVIATIONS

See page 93.

MAT

STRIP 1

Cast on 25 sts using US 3 (3.25 mm) needles and yarn A.

Cont in garter stitch as folls [ie. every row K]:-

4 rows using yarn A [for lower border].

18 rows using yarn B.

6 rows using yarn C.

6 rows using yarn D.

18 rows using yarn E.

6 rows using yarn C.

18 rows using yarn D.

6 rows using yarn B.

18 rows using yarn C.

6 rows using yarn A.

18 rows using yarn B.

5 rows using yarn A ending with WS facing for next row:-

Next row (WS): Using yarn A bind off knitwise [on WS - the last 6 rows form top border].

STRIP 2

Cast on 25 sts using US 3 (3.25 mm) needles and yarn A.

Cont in garter stitch as folls [ie. every row K]:-

4 rows using yarn A [for lower border].

18 rows using yarn F.

6 rows using yarn G.

6 rows using yarn H.

6 rows using yarn E.

6 rows using yarn H.

18 rows using yarn I.

6 rows using yarn H.

6 rows using yarn C.

18 rows using yarn G.

6 rows using yarn E.

6 rows using yarn H.
18 rows using yarn F.
5 rows using yarn A ending with WS facing for next row:-
Next row (WS): Using yarn A bind off knitwise [on WS - the last 6 rows form top border].

STRIP 3

Cast on 25 sts using US 3 (3.25 mm) needles and yarn A.
Cont in garter stitch as folls [ie. every row K]:-
4 rows using yarn A [for lower border].
18 rows using yarn G.
6 rows using yarn H.
18 rows using yarn E.
6 rows using yarn G.
6 rows using yarn A.
6 rows using yarn G.
18 rows using yarn E.
6 rows using yarn H.
6 rows using yarn F.
6 rows using yarn H.
6 rows using yarn F.
8 rows using yarn G.
5 rows using yarn A ending with WS facing for next row:-
Next row (WS): Using yarn A bind off knitwise [on WS - the last 6 rows form top border].

FINISHING

Matching the garter ridge-rows of each strip and using a neat mattress stitch to join strips together, join all 3 strips as shown in illustration.

SIDE EDGINGS [both alike]

With RS facing using US 3 (3.25 mm) needles and yarn A, pick up and Knit 70 sts along row end edge of mat.
Knit 4 rows ending with WS facing for next row.
Next row (WS): Cast off knitwise.

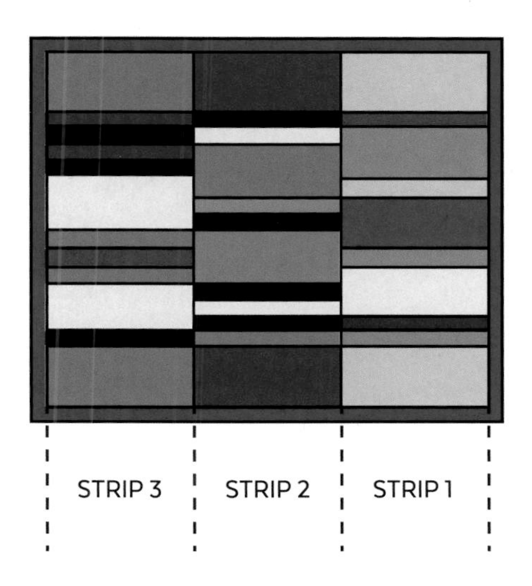

sunset pillow

YARN

Pure Wool Superwash Worsted

A	Charcoal Grey	155	2 x 3½oz/219yd balls
B	Light Denim	154	2 x 3½oz/219yd balls

OR

Pure Wool Superwash Worsted

A	Charcoal Grey	155	2 x 3½oz/219yd balls
B	Moonstone	112	2 x 3½oz/219yd balls

NEEDLES

1 pair US 7 (4.5mm) needles.

EXTRAS

17½ in (45 cm) square pillow form.

GAUGE

20 sts and 25 rows to 4in (10cm) square measured over stockinette stitch using US 7 (4.5mm) needles, or size required to obtain correct gauge.

FINISHED SIZE

Pillow measures approx 17½ in x17½ in (45 cm x 45 cm)

ABBREVIATIONS

See page 93.

NOTE

When working from Chart, right side rows are read from right to left; wrong side rows are read from left to right.

PILLOW FRONT

BLOCK 1 [make 5]

Cast on 30 sts using US 7 (4.5mm) needles and yarn A.
Cont to work from chart, beg at bottom right hand corner (1st row is RS of work) until all 47 rows have been worked changing colors when necessary and working the contrast areas of the circle using the Intarsia technique (i.e, use a separate ball/length of yarn for each block of color, twisting yarns together at WS of work when changing color), ending with WS facing for next row.
Bind off knitwise.

BLOCK 2 [make 4]

Cast on 30sts using US 7 (4.5mm) needles and yarn B.
Work as Block 1 using colors as stated on key for Block 2.

PILLOW BACK

Cast on 89 sts using US 7 (4.5mm) needles and yarn A.
Working in garter st throughout (i.e. knit every row).
Work the foll 4 row stripe sequence:-
Row 1 and 2: Using yarn A.
Row 3 and 4: Using yarn B.
Cont as set until pillow back meas 17½ in (45 cm) ending with WS facing for next row.
Bind off knitwise.

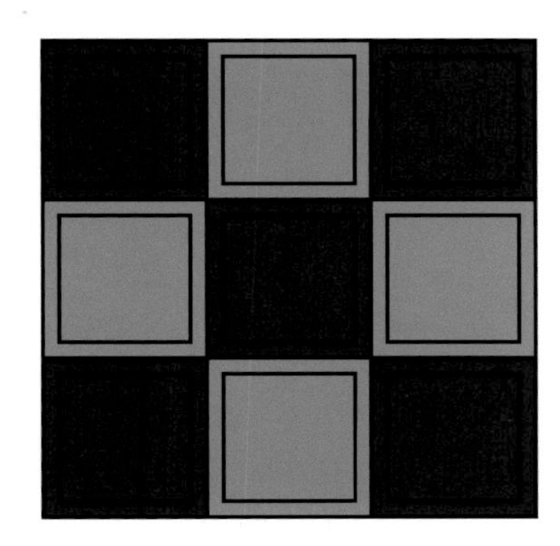

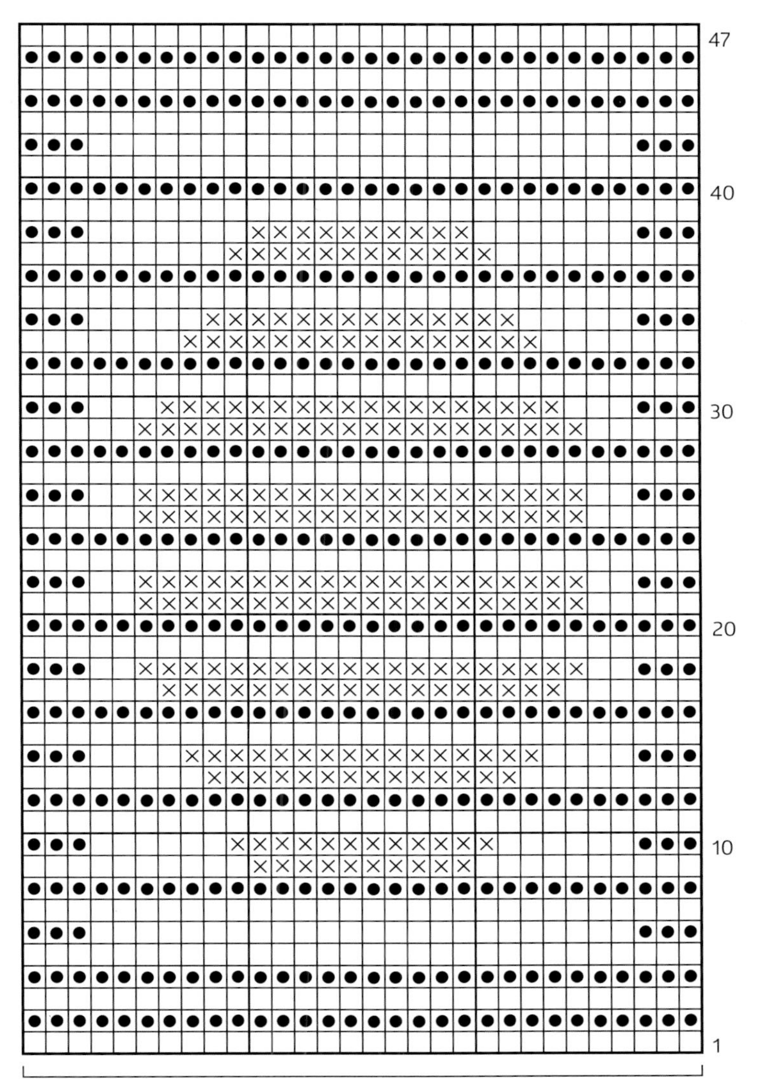

FINISHING

To form Pillow front: Join blocks as shown in diagram to form a square 3 blocks wide and 3 blocks long [9 blocks in total] with block 1 in each corner and at center.

Join both sides of pillow together using back stitch or mattress stitch if preferred, along 3 sides. Insert cushion pad, then close 4th side.

KEY

- ☐ Block 1: K on RS, P on WS in A
  Block 2: K on RS, P on WS in B
- ● Block 1: P on RS, K on WS in A
  Block 2: P on RS, K on WS in B
- ☒ Block 1: K on RS, P on WS in B
  Block 2: K on RS, P on WS in A

autumn leaves throw and runner

YARN

Felted Tweed

1 x 1¾oz/131yd ball of each of the following shades will be adequate to work both projects.

A	Mineral	181	
B	Tawny	186	
C	Camel	157	
D	Phantom	153	
E	Ginger	154	
F	Avocado	161	
G	Pine	158	
H	Clay	177	
(Used for throw only):			
I	Peony	183	2 x 1¾oz/131yd ball

NEEDLES

1 pair US 5 (3.75 mm) needles and US 2 (2.75 mm) needles

2 x US 2 (2.75 mm) double pointed needles

GAUGE

24 sts and 32 rows to 4in (10 mm) square measured over stockinette stitch using US 5 (3.75 mm) needles, or size required to obtain correct gauge.

FINISHED SIZE

Sofa throw without trim measures approx 15½ in (40 cm) x 31½ in (80 cm)

Runner measures approx. 8 in (20 cm) x 15½ in (40 cm)

ABBREVIATIONS

See page 93.

SOFA THROW

SQUARES

Make 4 squares in yarns A, B, C, D, E, F, G and H as folls:-

Cast on 24 sts using US 5 (3.75 mm) needles.

Work 32 rows in stockinette stitch (i.e - knit RS rows and purl WS rows), ending with RS facing for next row.

Bind off.

Total = 32 squares.

LEAF 1 (make 4)

Cast on 3 sts using US 2 (2.75 mm) double pointed needles and yarn G.

Stalk

Row 1 (RS): K3, *without turning work slip these 3 sts to opposite end of needle and bring yarn to opposite end of work pulling it quite tightly across back of these 3 sts. Using the other needle K these 3 sts again; rep from * 7 times more.

Main Leaf

Change to normal US 2 (2.75 mm) needles.

Row 1 (RS): K1, yfwd, K1, yfwd, K1, using yarn G. *5 sts.*

Row 2: K2, P1, K2, using yarn G.

When changing colors carry up the side of the work, taking the darker shade over the lighter color.

Row 3: K2, yfwd, K1, yfwd, K2, using yarn H. *7 sts.*

Row 4: K3, P1, K3 using yarn H.

Row 5: K3, yfwd, K1, yfwd, K3, using yarn G. *9 sts.*

Row 6: K4, P1, K4 using yarn G.

Row 7: K4, yfwd, K1, yfwd, K4, using yarn H. *11 sts.*

Row 8: K5, P1, K5 using yarn H.

Row 9: K5, yfwd, K1, yfwd, K5, using yarn G. *13 sts.*

Row 10: K6, P1, K6 using yarn G.

Row 11: K6, yfwd, K1, yfwd, K6, using yarn H. *15 sts.*
Row 12: K7, P1, K7 using yarn H.
Row 13: K7, yfwd, K1, yfwd, K7, using yarn G. *17 sts.*
Row 14: K8, P1, K8 using yarn G.
Row 15: ssk, K to last 2 sts, k2tog, using yarn H. *15 sts.*
Row 16: K to end using yarn H.
Row 17: ssk, K to last 2 sts, k2tog, using yarn G. *13 sts.*
Row 18: K to end using yarn G.
Row 19: ssk, K to last 2 sts, k2tog, using yarn H. *11 sts.*
Row 20: K to end using yarn H.
Row 21: ssk, K to last 2 sts, k2tog, using yarn G. *9 sts.*
Row 22: K to end using yarn G.
Row 23: ssk, K to last 2sts, k2tog, using yarn H. *7 sts.*
Row 24: K to end using yarn H.
Row 25: ssk, K to last 2 sts, k2tog, using yarn G. *5 sts.*
Row 26: K to end using yarn G.
Row 27: ssk, K to last 2 sts, k2tog, using yarn H. *3 sts.*
Row 28: K to end using yarn H.
Row 29: K3tog and fasten off.

LEAVES 2–8

Make 4 each of the following leaves as set by Leaf 1 and swopping colors as stated below;
Leaf 2: Use yarn A throughout.
Leaf 3: Replace yarn G with yarn B and yarn H with yarn F.
Leaf 4: Use yarn F throughout.
Leaf 5: Use yarn H throughout.
Leaf 6: Replace yarn G with yarn D and yarn H with yarn A.

Leaf 7: Use yarn C throughout.

Leaf 8: Replace yarn G with yarn E and yarn H with yarn C.

Total = 32 Leaves

FINISHING

Sew leaves to top of corresponding square (i.e leaf 1 with square 1). Squares 1-4 with "tip" of leaf pointing to bottom right hand corner of square, bending "stalk" slightly to the right. Remaining squares 5-8, with "tip" of leaf pointing to bottom left hand corner of square, bending "stalk" slightly to the left.

Using back stitch or mattress stitch if preferred, join all 32 squares as shown by diagram, to form a large rectangle 4 squares wide and 8 squares long.

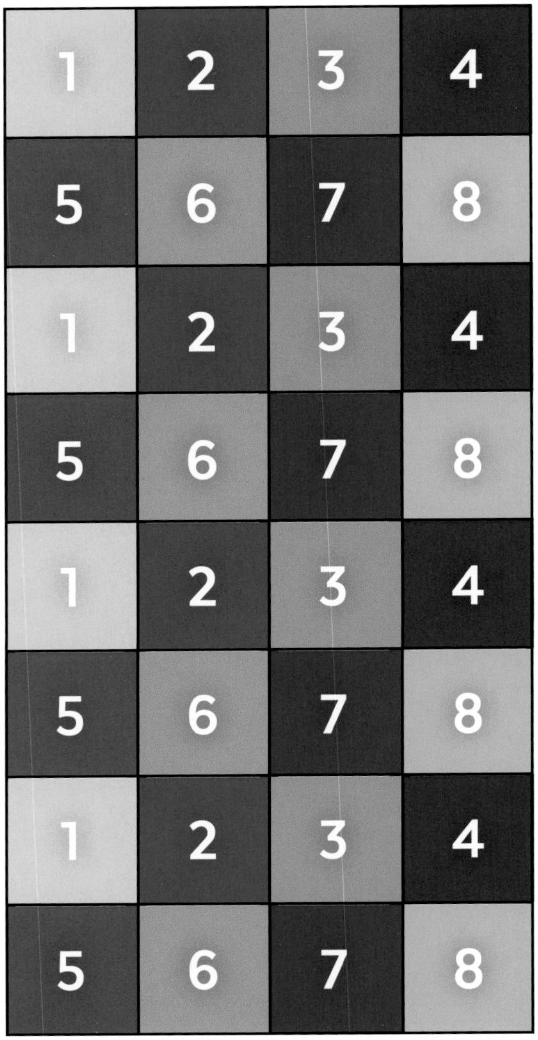

1	2	3	4
5	6	7	8
1	2	3	4
5	6	7	8
1	2	3	4
5	6	7	8
1	2	3	4
5	6	7	8

TRIM

Cast on 8 sts using US 2 (2.75 mm) needles and yarn I.

Row 1 (RS): K5, yfwd, K1, yfwd, K2.

Row 2: P6, inc in next st by knitting into front and back of it, K3.

Row 3: K4, P1, K2, yfwd, K1, yfwd, K3.

Row 4: P8, inc in next st, K4.

Row 5: K4, P2, K3, yfwd, K1, yfwd, K4.

Row 6: P10, inc in next st, K5.

Row 7: K4, P3, K4, yfwd, K1, yfwd, K5.

Row 8: P12, inc in next st, P6.

Row 9: K4, P4, sl1K, K1, psso, K7, k2tog, K1.

Row 10: P10, inc in next st, K7.

Row 11: K4, P5, sl1K, K1, psso, K5, K2tog, K1.

Row 12: P8, inc in next st, K2, P1, K5.

Row 13: K4, P1, K1, P4, sl1K, K1, psso, K3, k2tog, K1.

Row 14: P6, inc in next st, K3, P1, K5.

Row 15: K4, P1, K1, P5, sl1K, K1, psso, K1, k2tog, K1.

Row 16: P4, inc in next st, K4, P1, K5.

Row 17: K4, P1, K1, P6, sl1K, k2tog, psso, K1.

Row 18: P2tog, bind off 5 sts using the p2tog as the first of these sts (1 st on right hand needle), K1, P1, K5.

These 18 rows form the trim patt.

Cont to repeat these 18 rows until the trim fits around entire outer edge of throw, slip stitching straight edge of trim into place as you go along, slightly gathering the trim at the corners and ending after a full pattern repeat.

Bind off. Join cast-on and bound-off edges together.

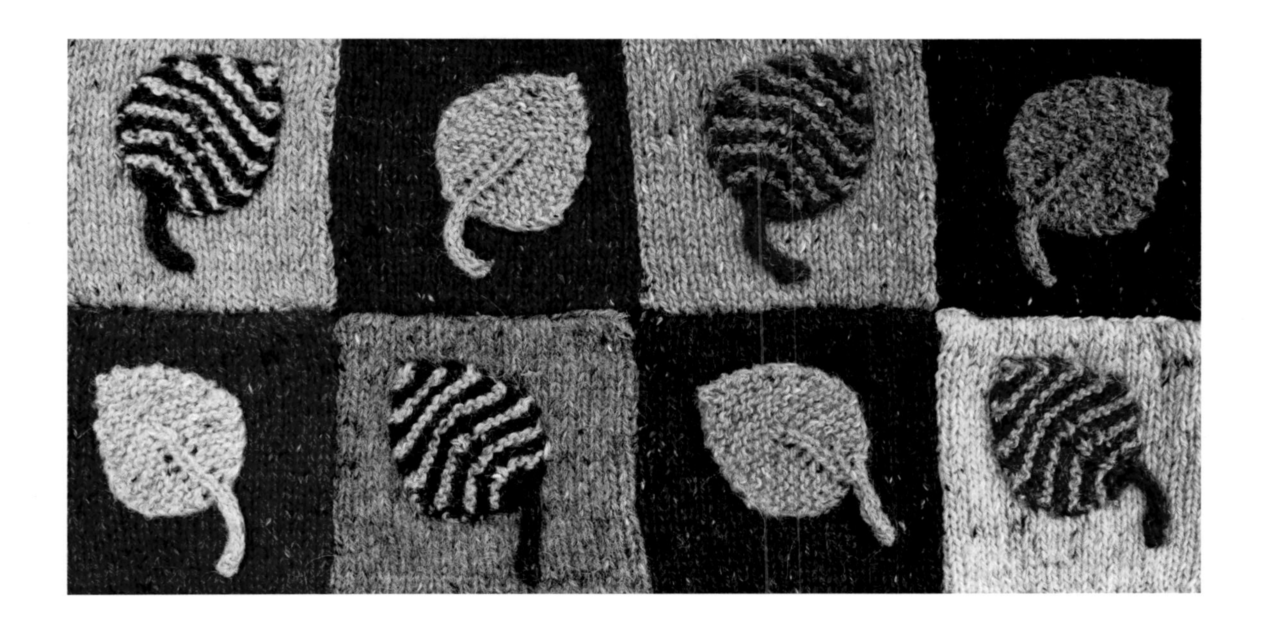

RUNNER

Work 1 square and 1 leaf in each colorway and attach leaves to squares as throw.

Total = 8 Squares

FINISHING

Using back stitch or mattress stitch if preferred join all 8 squares as shown by diagram, to form a rectangle 4 squares wide and 2 squares long.

RUNNER EDGING

Top and Bottom Edgings (both alike)

With RS facing using US 2 (2.75 mm) needles and yarn F, pick up and Knit 100sts along top (bound-off) edging or bottom (cast-on) edging.

Row 1 (RS): K to end.

Row 2: K1, m1, K to last st, m1, K1.

Rep the last 2 rows once more. *104 sts.*

Bind off.

Side Edgings (both alike)

With RS facing using US 2 (2.75 mm) needles and yarn F, pick up and Knit 50sts along row end edge.

Row 1 (RS): K to end.

Row 2: K1, m1, K to last st, m1, K1.

Rep the last 2 rows once more. *54 sts.*

Bind off.

Join corners of edgings.

1	2	3	4
5	6	7	8

useful information

GAUGE

Gauge controls both the shape and size of an article, so any variation, however slight, can distort the finished piece of knitting. To check your gauge, knit a square in the pattern stitch and/or stockinette stitch of perhaps 5-10 more stitches and 5-10 more rows than those given in the gauge note. Press the finished square under a damp cloth and mark out the central 4 in/10 cm square with pins. If you have more stitches to 4 in/10 cm than the given gauge, try again using bigger needles. If you have fewer stitches than the given gauge, try again using smaller needles. Once you have achieved the correct gauge, your project will be knitted to the measurements given.

CABLE PATTERNS

Cable stitch patterns allow you to twist the stitches in various ways to create decorative effects to give an interesting ropelike structure to the knitting. The cables can be thin and fine (just a couple of stitches wide) or big and chunky (up to 8 stitches or more). To work cables, you need to hold the appropriate number of stitches that form the cable twist (abbreviated in pattern as C) on a separate small cable needle, while you knit behind or in front of them. You then knit the stitches off the cable needle before continuing to knit the remaining stitches in the row. Depending on whether the cable needle is at the front or the back of the work, the cables will twist to the left or right but the principle remains the same. A four-stitch cable will be abbreviated as c4f or c4b, depending on whether the cable needle is held to the front or back of the work. Abbreviations for the variations of cable, cross and twisted stitches are given in each pattern.

FAIR ISLE

When you are working a pattern with two or more repeating colors in the same row, you need to strand the yarn not in use behind the stitches being worked. This needs to be done with care, loosely enough to ensure that the strands not in use do not tighten and pucker the front of the knitting. To do this you need to treat the yarns not in use, known as "floating yarns", as if they were one yarn and spread the stitches as you work to their correct width to keep them elastic. If you tend to knit colorwork too tightly, increase your needle size for the colorwork section.

INTARSIA

This allows you to join in new yarns in the middle of rows where a new color extends over more than 5 stitches or so. The simplest method is to cut short lengths of yarn for each block of color and bind each them into small bobbins. Work across the row, joining in colors from bobbins as required, twisting them around each other on the WS of the work to avoid any gaps. After you have completed the piece of knitting, neaten up the loose ends by darning along the color joins. When working in Intarsia, check that the tension is correct; it may vary from the plain stockinette stitch if both are used in the pattern.

FINISHING METHODS

Pressing

Block out each piece of knitting by pinning it on a board to the correct measurements in the pattern. Then lightly press it according to the ball band instructions, omitting any ribbed areas. Take special care to press the edges, as this makes sewing up easier and neater. If you cannot press the fabric, then cover the knitted fabric with a damp cloth and allow it to stand for a couple of hours. Darn in all ends neatly along the selvedge edge or a color join.

Stitching seams

When you stitch the pieces together, remember to match any areas of color and texture carefully where they meet. Using a special seam stitch, called mattress stitch, creates the neatest flattest seam. After all the seams are complete, press the seams and hems. Lastly, sew on the buttons to correspond with the positions of the buttonholes.

ABBREVIATIONS

alt	alternate
approx	approximately
beg	begin(s)(ning)
cm	centimeters
cont	continu(e)(ing)
dec	decreas(e)(ing)
foll(s)	follow(s)(ing)
g	gram
g-st	garter stitch
in	inch(es)
inc	increas(e)(ing)
K	knit
k2tog	knit next 2 sts together
k3tog	knit next 3 sts together
mm	millimeters
m1	make one st by picking up horizontal loop before next st and knitting into back of it
patt	pattern
P	purl
psso	pass slipped stitch over
p2tog	purl next 2 sts together
rem	remain(s)(ing)
rep	repeat
RS	right side
skpo	sl 1, k1, pass slipped stitch over
sk2po	sl 1, knit 2 together, pass slipped stitch over
sl 1	slip one st
st(s)	stitch(es)
St st	stockinette stitch (1 row knit, 1 row purl)
tbl	through back of loop(s)
tog	together
WS	wrong side
yd	yard(s)
yfwd	yarn forward
yo	yarn over
ytf	with yarn to front
ytb	with yarn to back
[ ]/*	repeat instructions within square brackets or between asterisk

ACKNOWLEDGMENTS

A big, big thank you to the following team of people: Steven and Susan for their wonderful photography, art direction and styling; Anne for working her usual magic on the fabulous layouts and for the charts; Frances Jago for the beautifully knitted swatches and projects; Lisa for her diligent editing and checking; Ed for his diagrams; Sharon, David and the entire Rowan team for their continuous support; and, last but not least, Penny and Lee for allowing us to take pictures in their stylish Ilfracombe home.

stockists

AUSTRALIA
Australian Country Spinners, Pty Ltd, Level 7, 409 St. Kilda Road, Melbourne Vic 3004.
Tel: 03 9380 3888 Fax: 03 9820 0989
Email: customerservice@auspinners.com.au

AUSTRIA
MEZ Harlander GmbH, Schulhof 6, 1. Stock, 1010 Wien, Austria
Tel: +00800 26 27 28 00 Fax: (00) 49 7644 802-133
Email: verkauf.harlander@mezcrafts.com Web: www.mezcrafts.at

BELGIUM
MEZ crafts Belgium NV, c/o MEZ GmbH, Kaiserstr.1, 79341 Kenzingen, Germany
Tel: 0032 (0) 800 77 89 2 Fax: 00 49 7644 802 133
Email: sales.be-nl@mezcrafts.com Web: www.mezcrafts.be

BULGARIA
MEZ Crafts Bulgaria EOOD, Bul. Rozhen 25A, BG-1220 Sofia, Bulgaria
Tel: +359 2 439 24 24 Fax: +359 2 439 24 28
Email: office.bg@mezcrafts.com

CANADA
Westminster Fibers, 10 Roybridge Gate, Suite 200, Vaughan, Ontario L4H 3M8
Tel: (800) 263-2354 Fax: 905-856-6184
Email: info@westminsterfibers.com

CHINA
Commercial agent Mr Victor Li, c/o MEZ GmbH Germany, Kaiserstr. 1, 79341 Kenzingen, Germany
Tel: (86- 21) 13816681825 Email: victor.li@mezcrafts.com

CHINA
SHANGHAI YUJUN CO.,LTD., Room 701 Wangjiao Plaza, No.175 Yan'an(E), 200002 Shanghai, China
Tel: +86 2163739785 Email: jessechang@vip.163.com

CYPRUS
MEZ Crafts Bulgaria EOOD, Bul. Rozhen 25A, BG-1220 Sofia, Bulgaria
Tel: +359 2 439 24 24 Fax: +359 2 439 24 28
Email: office.bg@mezcrafts.com

CZECH REPUBLIC
Coats Czecho s.r.o.Staré Mesto 246 569 32
Tel: (420) 461616633 Email: galanterie@coats.com

DENMARK
Carl J. Permin A/S Egegaardsvej 28 DK-2610 Rødovre
Tel: (45) 36 72 12 00 E-mail: permin@permin.dk

ESTONIA
MEZ Crafts Estonia OÜ, Ampri tee 9/4, 74001 Viimsi Harjumaa
Tel: +372 630 6252 Email: info.ee@mezcrafts.com
Web: www.coatscrafts.co.ee

FINLAND
MEZ Crafts Finland Oy, Huhtimontie 6, 04200 Kerava
Tel: (358) 9 274 871 Email: sales.fi@mezcrafts.com
Web: www.coatscrafts.fi

FRANCE
3bcom, 35 avenue de Larrieu, 31094 Toulouse cedex 01
Tel: 0033 (0) 562 202 096 Email: Commercial@3b-com.com

GERMANY
MEZ GmbH, Kaiserstr. 1, 79341 Kenzingen
Tel: 0049 7644 802 222 Email: kenzingen.vertrieb@mezcrafts.com
Fax: 0049 7644 802 300 Web: www.mezcrafts.de

GREECE
MEZ Crafts Bulgaria EOOD, Bul. Rozhen 25A, BG-1220 Sofia, Bulgaria
Tel: +359 2 439 24 24 Fax: +359 2 439 24 28
Email: office.bg@mezcrafts.com

HOLLAND
G. Brouwer & Zn B.V., Oudhuijzerweg 69, 3648 AB Wilnis, Netherlands
Tel: 0031 (0) 297-281 557 Email: info@gbrouwer.nl

HONG KONG
East Unity Company Ltd, Unit B2, 7/F., Block B, Kailey Industrial Centre, 12 Fung Yip Street, Chai Wan
Tel: (852)2869 7110 Email: eastunityco@yahoo.com.hk

ICELAND
Carl J. Permin A/S Egegaardsvej 28 DK-2610 Rødovre
Tel: (45) 36 72 12 00 Email: permin@permin.dk

ITALY
Mez Cucirini Italy Srl, Viale Sarca, 223, 20126 MILANO
Tel: 02 636151 Fax: 02 66111701

JAPAN
Hobbyra Hobbyre Corporation, 23-37, 5-Chome, Higashi-Ohi, Shinagawa-Ku, 1400011 Tokyo.
Tel: +81334721104
Daidoh International, 3-8-11 Kudanminami Chiyodaku, Hiei Kudan Bldg 5F, 1018619 Tokyo.
Tel: +81-3-3222-7076 Fax: +81-3-3222-7066

KOREA
My Knit Studio, 3F, 144 Gwanhun-Dong, 110-300 Jongno-Gu, Seoul
Tel: 82-2-722-0006 Email: myknit@myknit.com
Web: www.myknit.com

LATVIA
Coats Latvija SIA, Mukusalas str. 41 b, Riga LV-1004
Tel: +371 67 625173 Fax: +371 67 892758
Email: info.latvia@coats.com Web: www.coatscrafts.lv

LEBANON
y.knot, Saifi Village, Mkhalissiya Street 162, Beirut
Tel: (961) 1 992211 Fax: (961) 1 315553 Email: y.knot@cyberia.net.lb

LITHUANIA and RUSSIA
MEZ Crafts Lithuania UAB, A. Juozapaviciaus str. 6/2,
LT-09310 Vilnius
Tel: +370 527 30971 Fax: +370 527 2305
Email: info.lt@mezcrafts.com Web: www.coatscrafts.lt

LUXEMBOURG
Coats N.V., c/o Coats GmbH, Kaiserstr.1, 79341 Kenzingen, Germany
Tel: 00 49 7644 802 222 Fax: 00 49 7644 802 133
Email: sales.coatsninove@coats.com Web: www.coatscrafts.be

MEXICO
Estambres Crochet SA de CV, Aaron Saenz 1891-7Pte, 64650
MONTERREY
Tel: +52 (81) 8335-3870 Email: abremer@redmundial.com.mx

NEW ZEALAND
ACS New Zealand, P.O Box 76199, Northwood, Christchurch
Tel: 64 3 323 6665 Fax: 64 3 323 6660 Email: lynn@impactmg.
co.nz

NORWAY
Carl J. Permin A/S Egegaardsvej 28 DK-2610 Rødovre
Tel: (45) 36 72 12 00 E-mail: permin@permin.dk

PORTUGAL
Mez Crafts Portugal, Lda - Av. Vasco da Gama, 774-4431-059 V.N,
Gaia
Tel: 00 351 223 770700 Email: sales.iberia@mezcrafts.com

SINGAPORE
Golden Dragon Store, BLK 203 Henderson Rd #07-02, 159546
Henderson Indurstrial Park
Tel: (65) 62753517 Fax: (65) 62767112 Email: gdscraft@hotmail.
com

SLOVAKIA
MEZ Crafts Slovakia, s.r.o. Seberíniho 1, 821 03 Bratislava
Tel: +421 2 32 30 31 19 Email: galanteria@mezcrafts.com

SOUTH AFRICA
Arthur Bales LTD, 62 4th Avenue, Linden 2195
Tel: (27) 11 888 2401 Fax: (27) 11 782 6137
Email: arthurb@new.co.za
Web: www.arthurbales.co.za

SPAIN
MEZ Fabra Spain S.A, Avda Meridiana 350, pta 13 D,
08027 Barcelona
Tel: +34 932908400 Fax: +34 932908409
Email: atencion.clientes@mezcrafts.com

SWEDEN
Carl J. Permin A/S Egegaardsvej 28 DK-2610 Rødovre
Tel: (45) 36 72 12 00 Email: permin@permin.dk

SWITZERLAND
MEZ Crafts Switzerland GmbH, Stroppelstrasse20,
5417 Untersiggenthal
Tel: +41 00800 2627 2800 Fax: 0049 7644 802 133
Email: verkauf.ch@mezcrafts.com Web: www.mezcrafts.ch

TURKEY
MEZ Crafts Tekstil A.S, Kavacık Mahallesi, Ekinciler Cad. Necip Fazıl
Sok.
No.8 Kat: 5, 34810 Beykoz/Istanbul
Tel: +90 216 425 88 10 Web: www.mezcrafts.com

TAIWAN
Cactus Quality Co Ltd, 7FL-2, No. 140, Sec.2 Roosevelt Rd, Taipei,
10084 Taiwan, R.O.C.
Tel: 00886-2-23656527 Fax: 886-2-23656503
Email: cqcl@ms17.hinet.net

THAILAND
Global Wide Trading, 10 Lad Prao Soi 88, Bangkok 10310
Tel: 00 662 933 9019 Fax: 00 662 933 9110
Email: global.wide@yahoo.com

U.S.A.
Westminster Fibers, 8 Shelter Drive, Greer, South Carolina, 29650
Tel: (800) 445-9276 Fax: 864-879-9432
Email: info@westminsterfibers.com

U.K
Coats Crafts UK, Green Lane Mill, Holmfirth, West Yorkshire,
England HD9 2DX
Tel: +44 (0) 1484 681881 Fax: +44 (0) 1484 687920
Email: ccuk.sales@coats.com Web: www.knitrowan.com

For more stockists in all countries please visit www.rowan.com

YARNS

The following Rowan yarns have been used in this book:

Alpaca Color
Alpaca: 100%; 1¾oz/50g balls; 131 yd/120 m per ball; 22 sts and 30 rows over 4 in/10 cm using US 6 (4 mm) needles.

Big Wool
100% Merino wool; 100g balls; 87 yd/80 m per ball; 7½-9 sts and 10-12½ rows over 4 in/10 cm using US 15 (10 mm) needles.

Creative Focus Worsted
75% wool; 25% alpaca;100g balls; 220 yd/200 m per ball; 20 sts and 24 rows to 4 in/10 cm using US 7 (4.5 mm) needles.

Felted Tweed
Merino Wool: 50%; Alpaca: 25%; Viscose: 25%; 1¾oz/50g balls; 191 yd/175 m per ball; 22-24 sts and 30-32 rows to 4 in/10 cm using US 5-6 (3.75-4 mm) needles.

Felted Tweed Aran
Merino Wool: 50%, Alpaca: 25%, Viscose: 25%; 1¾oz/50g balls; 95yd/87m per ball; 16 sts and 23 rows to 4 in/10 cm using US 8 (5 mm) needles.

Hemp Tweed
Wool: 75%; True Hemp: 25%; 1¾oz/50g balls; 104yd/95m per ball; 19 sts and 25 rows to 14 in/10 cm using US 7 (4.5 mm) needles.

Pure Wool DK
100 per cent Superwash Wool; 1¾oz/50g balls; 142yd /130m per ball; 22 sts and 30 rows to 4 in/ 10 cm using US 6 (4 mm) needles.

Pure Wool Superwash Worsted
Superwash Wool: 100%; 100g balls; 219 yd/200 m per ball; 20 sts and 25 rows over 4 in/10 cm using US 7 (4.5 mm) needles.

Summerlite 4 ply
Cotton: 100%: 1¾oz/50g balls; 191yd/175m per ball; 28 sts and 36 rows over 4 in/10 cm using US 2-3 (3 mm) needles.

Superfine Merino 4 ply
Merino wool: 100%; 1¾oz/50g balls; 181yd/165m per ball; 28 sts and 36 rows over 4 in/10 cm using US 3 (3.25 mm) needles.

Superwash Wool 100%
100g balls; 219yd/200m per ball; 20 sts and 25 rows to 4 in/10 cm using US 7 (4.5 mm) needles.

Wool Cotton
Cotton: 50%, Merino Wool: 50 per cent 1¾oz/50g balls; 124yd/113m per ball; 22-24 sts and 30-32 rows over 4 in/10 cm using US 5-6 (3.75-4 mm) needles.

Wool Cotton 4 ply
Cotton: 50%, Merino Wool: 50%; 1¾oz/50g balls; 197yd/180m per ball; 28 sts and 36 rows over 4 in/10 cm using US 3 (3.25 mm) needles.